# ANDREWS UNIVERSITY MONOGRAPHS

JAMES J. C. COX

*General Editor*


## STUDIES IN RELIGION

LAWRENCE T. GERATY

*Editor*


## ANDREWS UNIVERSITY MONOGRAPHS:
## STUDIES IN RELIGION

1. Alger F. Johns, *A Short Grammar of Biblical Aramaic*, 1963 (revised edition, 1966).

2. Roger S. Boraas and Siegfried H. Horn, *Heshbon 1968: The First Campaign at Tell Ḥesbân, A Preliminary Report*, 1969.

3. H. K. LaRondelle, *Perfection and Perfectionism: A Dogmatic-Ethical Study of Biblical Perfection and Phenomenal Perfectionism*, 1971 (second edition, 1975).

4. Sakae Kubo, *A Reader's Greek-English Lexicon of the New Testament*, 1967 (revised, enlarged edition, 1975).

5. Gerhard F. Hasel, *The Remnant: The History and Theology of the Remnant Idea from Genesis to Isaiah*, 1972 (second edition, 1974).

6. Roger S. Boraas and Siegfried H. Horn, *Heshbon 1971: The Second Campaign at Tell Ḥesbân, A Preliminary Report*, 1973.

7. James A. Sauer, *Heshbon Pottery 1971: A Preliminary Report on the Pottery from the 1971 Excavations at Tell Ḥesbân*, 1973.

8. Roger S. Boraas and Siegfried H. Horn, *Heshbon 1973: The Third Campaign at Tell Ḥesbân, A Preliminary Report*, 1975.

ANDREWS UNIVERSITY MONOGRAPHS

STUDIES IN RELIGION

VOLUME VIII

# HESHBON 1973

## THE THIRD CAMPAIGN AT *TELL ḤESBÂN*

### A PRELIMINARY REPORT

BY

ROGER S. BORAAS AND SIEGFRIED H. HORN

*With Contributions by*
Dewey M. Beegle, Frank Moore Cross, Lawrence T. Geraty,
Robert Ibach, Jr., Øystein and Asta Sakala LaBianca,
James A. Sauer, Henry O. Thompson, Bastiaan Van Elderen,
S. Douglas Waterhouse

ANDREWS UNIVERSITY PRESS
BERRIEN SPRINGS, MICHIGAN
1975

*Reprinted from:*

## ANDREWS UNIVERSITY SEMINARY STUDIES

Volume XIII, Numbers 1 and 2, 1975

Printed by University Printers, Berrien Springs, Michigan, USA

# CONTENTS

Page

## APPENDIX

Page

## TEXT FIGURES

Figure      Page

## TABLES

# PLATES

(After page 248)

## APPENDIX: PLATES

(After page 22)

ANDREWS UNIVERSITY

# HESHBON EXPEDITION

## THE THIRD CAMPAIGN AT *TELL ḤESBÂN* (1973)

ROGER S. BORAAS
Upsala College
East Orange, N.J.

SIEGFRIED H. HORN
Andrews University
Berrien Springs, Mich.

The third campaign at *Tell Ḥesbân* was conducted from June 20 to August 14, 1973.[1] Heshbon's history from literary sources and a description of *Tell Ḥesbân* and its geographical location[2] have already been covered in previous reports. For this reason these will not be discussed in this report.

### *Organization*

Andrews University was again the major sponsor of the expedition, but sizable subventions were once more made by Calvin Theological Seminary, Grand Rapids, Michigan, and the American Center for Oriental Research in Amman (ACOR) thanks to the generosity of the late ACOR board member H. Dunscombe Colt. Smaller contributions came from several private individuals. Again a word of thanks is due to all those who, through their financial support, made the expedition possible and thus shared in its success.

As in 1971 the headquarters were in the American Com-

[1] For the 1968 season, see R. S. Boraas and S. H. Horn, *et al.*, *Heshbon 1968* (*AUSS*, 7 [1969]: 97-239); AUM, Vol. 2, 1969; Horn, *ADAJ*, 12-13 (1967-1968): 51-52; Horn, *BA*, 32 (1969): 26-41; Horn, *RB*, 76 (1969): 395-398; A. Terian, "Coins from the 1968 Excavation at Heshbon," *AUSS*, 9 (1971): 147-160; E. N. Lugenbeal and J. A. Sauer, "Seventh-sixth Century B.C. Pottery from Area B at Heshbon," *AUSS*, 10 (1972): 21-69.

For the 1971 season, see R. S. Boraas and S. H. Horn, *et al.*, *Heshbon 1971* (*AUSS*, 11 [1973]: 1-144), AUM, 6, 1973; Horn, *ADAJ*, 17 (1972): 15-22; Horn, *RB*, 79 (1972): 422-426; R. G. Bullard, "Geological Study of the Heshbon Area," *AUSS*, 10 (1972): 129-141; J. A. Sauer, *Heshbon Pottery 1971* (AUM, Vol. 7, 1973); A. Terian, "Coins from the 1971 Excavations at Heshbon," *AUSS*, 12 (1974): 35-46.

[2] W. Vyhmeister, *AUSS*, 6 (1968): 158-177; Boraas and Horn, *Heshbon 1968*, pp. 97-98.

munity School on the western outskirts of Amman. The
school plant was graciously placed at the disposal of the expedition by the school board through the good offices of its
chairman, Richard Undeland of the United States Embassy in
Amman. It provided once more excellent facilities for housing
most of the staff members and kitchen personnel, and for the
various archaeological headquarters activities.

The staff of 59 consisted of 49 overseas members and 10
Jordanians. The foreigners came from the United States of
America, Canada, Germany, Norway, South Africa and Australia.
Nearly half of them were students. The host country was repre-
sented by several members of the staff of the Department of
Antiquities and students of the University of Jordan who had
majored in archaeology.

The director of the expedition was again Siegfried H. Horn.
Roger S. Boraas served once more as the expedition's chief
archaelogist. Their responsibilities were the same as in previous
seasons. Continuity in staff assignments was achieved to a great
extent by the fact that seven members had been with the expedition from its beginning in 1968, while another 17 members served
the Heshbon expedition for the second season in 1973. In the
following list staff members are mentioned in connection with
their major assignments, although a few shifts took place during
the season.

Area A, on the summit of the acropolis where the remains of
a Byzantine church had been discovered in 1968, was once more
supervised by Bastiaan Van Elderen, who from 1972-1974 served
in Amman as the director of ACOR. Work continued here in three
of the six Squares previously opened while two new Squares were
opened in the western part of the Area. The Square supervisors of
Area A were Emmet A. Barnes, Douglas R. Clark, Ann O. Koloski,
Paul E. Moore, and Eric C. Schilperoort.

Area B, on the shelf below and south of the acropolis, stood
again under the supervision of James A. Sauer, who as the

expedition's pottery expert was also responsible for all pottery reading. Since it was anticipated that the new Square D.4 which lies between Squares B.3 and D.3 would correlate more closely to the Squares B.1-3, this new Square was also under Sauer's supervision, as well as two minor soundings (labeled B.5 and B.6), north and west of Squares B.1 and B.2. The Square supervisors of Area B were Adil Abu Shmais, James R. Battenfield, Susan A. Hamilton, Norman Johnson, Philip J. Post, David Undeland, and Udo Worschech. In Square D.4 Elizabeth G. Burr and Samir Ghishan served as supervisors.

For Area C, on the western slope of the *tell*, the work was continued in three of the five Squares previously excavated. Henry O. Thompson served as supervisor of this Area as in both previous seasons. The Square supervisors of Area C were B. Michael Blaine, Ibrahim Hajj Hasan, Nabil Salim Qadi, Thomas J. Meyer, Omar Daoud, and Douglas J. Stek.

Area D, which covered the remains of the ascent to the summit from the south and which lay between Areas A and B, was again supervised by Lawrence T. Geraty. Work was continued in all five Squares previously opened. The Square supervisors of Area D were Ali Musa, Jack B. Bohannon, Lillian A. Foster, Lutfi Ostah, Richard C. Mannell, Julia Neuffer, Catherine Schilperoort, and John W. Wood.

Work in the Roman-Byzantine Cemetery F on the southwestern slope of *Tell Ḥesbân* was continued and several new tombs were discovered. Dewey M. Beegle, the supervisor, was assisted by Timothy Smith, Mary Stek, Anita Van Eldern and Donald H. Wimmer.

G was the Area designation for several soundings made at different places on the *tell* and in a cave at its western slope. Dewey M. Beegle also supervised these probes and was assisted by Ghazzan Ramakhe and Leonard P. Tolhurst.

The archaeological and topographical survey team which explored the area around *Tell Ḥesbân* was headed by S. Douglas

Waterhouse. He was assisted by B. Charlene Hogsten and Robert D. Ibach, while the following staff members served part time in this project: Ali Musa, Eugenia L. Nitowski, and Sami Abadi.

Bert De Vries, Albright Fellow of ACOR for 1972-1973, served the expedition for the third time as surveyor and architect. His assistant was Gary Roozeboom. Mary Stek helped as draftswoman. They continued the survey of the *tell* and its surroundings (see Contour Map, Fig. 1), made plans and elevations of all architectural remains as these were excavated, and were frequently called upon to provide levels for various excavated features.

As in 1968, Avery V. Dick was chief photographer. His assistants were Paul J. Bergsma and James H. Zachary. Eugenia L. Nitowski helped with the darkroom chores.

Øystein LaBianca, assisted by his wife Asta, was the expedition's anthropologist and was responsible for the animal bone material, while Eugenia L. Nitowski took care of the human skeletal material.

Hester Thomsen was again responsible for all pottery operations in camp, which included supervising of the washing, drying and sorting of all sherds retrieved during the excavations, and the registration of the more than 30,000 sherds retained for further study. Aina E. Boraas used her skills to restore pottery as much as possible.

Marion E. Beegle was registrar of objects, and Elizabeth C. Sanford served as conservator. It was the first time that the expedition enjoyed the presence of a professional conservator on its staff.

The camp director was once more Vivolyn Van Elderen. Mohammad Adawi, the major-domo of ACOR, served just as in previous seasons as the expedition's cook. He had four assistants.

All legible coins were identified by Abraham Terian. His 1973 coin article is scheduled for a future number of the *AUSS*.

The Department of Antiquities, which through Director-

General Yacoub Oweis issued the excavation permit, was as usual most helpful in many ways. Mohammad Murshed Khadija, one of the department's officials, was loaned to the expedition and once more served as its foreman, mainly in charge of the 130 villagers hired as local laborers. Ali Musa and Ibrahim Hajj Hasan were assigned as the department's representatives and served also in other capacities, as has already been mentioned above. Thanks are also due to Mr. Oweis for having secured a permit for conducting the regional survey, for loaning equipment to the expedition when needed, and for various other courtesies extended. Much of the success and the smooth operation of the expedition is due to the cooperation and helpfulness of the officials of this department in general and to Mr. Oweis in particular.

### Aims[3]

Since it was possible that the 1973 season would be the last season of the Andrews University excavations at *Tell Ḥesbân,* all decisions concerning field tactics were conditioned by this possibility. For this reason portions of some Squares were reduced in the hope to reach bedrock along the fullest possible extent of the main east-west and north-south axes as well as along the north balk of Area B. It was anticipated that in this way we might obtain the most complete stratigraphic record of the three seasons of work on the site. In addition, special problems received specific attention, such as the western dimensions of the Byzantine Church on the acropolis, the occupational stratigraphy on the eastern slope of the *tell,* location of the Roman road "from Esbus to Livias," the search for additional tombs, the location of outlying settlements in the immediately adjacent

[3] The strategy, methods, and techniques employed were essentially the same as in the previous seasons and their description needs therefore no repetition (see *Heshbon 1968,* pp. 110-117). It may be repeated here that the letters A-G stand for Areas A-G; the first numeral after these letters, for the number of the Square referred to; and the following numeral preceded by a colon to the locus number; hence A.3:14 means Area A, Square 3, Locus 14, while D.6 refers merely to Area D, Square 6.

region, and the improvement of ecological data-gathering and artifact conservation in the field.

## Accomplishments

We shall summarize the work of the 1973 season by reporting only the new material found for each of the periods involved, beginning with the earliest.[4] It is assumed that the reader is acquainted with the accomplishments of the two preceding seasons.

*Iron I* (1200-900 B.C.) Stratified materials occurred in Areas B and C, with miscellaneous sherds from the Iron I period recovered just over bedrock in the sounding G.1. In Square C.1 such remains appeared to be in dump layers lying just above bedrock. In Area B there appeared structures which seemed to be three walls crossing a declivity in bedrock. They enclosed some mixed soil and ash layers in which Iron I pottery was found. The precise functions of these walls did not yet become apparent, but the soil sequences and ceramics involved suggested domestic settlement. The pottery evidence indicated that these remains belonged to the early Iron I period.

*Iron II/Persian* (ca. 700-500 B.C.). Stratified materials were found in Areas B and C, with sherds in mixed loci in Area D. On the west slope a few soil layers were dated to this period in Square C. 1, but the first elements of what seemed to be possible Iron Age defense structures occurred further up the slope (Squares C.3 and possibly C.2) in the form of major buttressed masonry following the contour of the bedrock on which it was founded. Only foundation courses remained to be traceable, the super-

---

[4] Period divisions adopted for this report follow the scheme worked out by James A. Sauer, *Heshbon Pottery 1971*, pp. 1-7. Stratum designations with Arabic numerals have been adopted by the authors of reports on Areas B and D as means of distinguishing the accumulated stratification within each respective Area. Hence the numerical sequences vary from one Area to the other, consequently designating remains of different periods in some instances. Designation of Strata by Roman numerals is reserved for site-wide Stratum identifications, as indicated in *Heshbon 1968*, pp. 114-115.

structures having long since fallen or been removed by later occupants.

The most notable structural remains in Area B from this period were parts of a thick cement floor in Square B.1 and parts of a possible retaining wall in Squares B.2 and 4 of a large open-air reservoir on the south shelf of the *tell*. The floor comprised three superimposed layers of cement over bedrock, the top of which was nearly level. The possible eastern retaining wall of this installation consisted in part of the plastered faces of bedrock cut vertically and in part of a contiguous well-built header-stretcher wall of which a 16.00 m. length was exposed in Squares B.2 and 4 without reaching its corners. The season's work allowed no more than the exposure of eight courses of the header-stretcher wall and of the comparable depth of the faces of the bedrock portions of the reservoir's eastern retaining wall. The dates for the construction of this installation and its most recent use—7th and 6th cent. B.C.—were determined on the basis of the few sherds retrieved from the wall and cement, and from ample ceramics in the layer of clay lying just above the cement floor. The available time did not allow us to ascertain the size of the installation, nor whether the cement floor and plastered retaining wall were connected.

The discovery of this installation reminds one of the fact that the Biblical Heshbon was famous for its pools at the gate of Bath-rabbim, as attested in Song of Solomon 7:4. Only future excavations may show whether the installation of Area B can be one of the pools mentioned in the Bible.

*Early Hellenistic* (332-198 B.C.). The only trace of occupation from this period was what seemed to be a layer of fill laid over bedrock in the sounding G.1 on the east slope of the *tell*. This layer, also containing some Iron Age I sherds, may have been the makeup for a plaster surface.

*Late Hellenistic* (198-63 B.C.) Extensive evidence from this period was recovered in Areas B and D, with supplemental material in Area C. Squares B.1, 2 and 4 contained a massive accumulation of soil layers which had been produced by filling in the "reservoir" after it was abandoned. While the bulk of the pottery evidence from these layers came from the Iron II/Persian period, it became clear that Hellenistic settlers were responsible for this fill when an indisputable Hellenistic sherd was found in a non-intrusive locus near the bottom of the accumulated soil layers. The depth and volume of this fill suggested that the settlers had conducted extensive clearing operations of earlier occupational debris over sizable portions of the *tell*, possibly the acropolis.

Evidence of their domestic facilities included storage pits cut into bedrock and some storage jars found in Area B, while clues to a somewhat sparse and perhaps temporary habitation in Area C were provided by a possible hearth and a firepit. Various evidences of Hellenistic remains in Area D also suggested that the occupants of this period used considerable portions of the site.

That they intended to keep control of the site is most clearly apparent in the major masonry they constructed in Areas B and D. It seems that Hellenistic occupants constructed the first of a series of phases of a major defense wall surrounding the acropolis. This wall, D.1:4, was set firmly on bedrock and was nearly two meters thick. Similarly impressive wall foundations were dug into the "reservoir" fill by later occupants of the south shelf of the *tell*. Wall B.1:17 = B.2:62 with its conspicuous foundation trenches is also of a size that suggests defensive purposes. Problems attended both these constructions thus interpreted, as the details reported below will make clear, but these walls represent the most massive masonry erected on the site up to that time as far as our present evidence goes. One of these walls, D.1:4, continued to serve the occupants of Heshbon for centuries. Only scattered sherds were found in Area A (Square 6) from this period, suggesting that later clearing operations may have removed existing remains of the Hellenistic period.

*Early Roman* (63 B.C-A.D. 135). This period is represented at Esbus, as Heshbon was called in the Roman period, by a more diverse and widely dispersed range of evidence than any earlier period.

In Area A where the column support wall of the Byzantine church rested on foundations constructed in the Early Roman period, additional wall foundations were found. At the end of the 1973 season it was still unclear what functions some of these walls had performed. Concern to maintain an adequate water supply in the acropolis may have led to the construction of Cistern D.6:33. It was cut in bedrock and fitted with a neck built of ringed header stones.

There may have been an attempt to buttress the perimeter wall (D.1:4) around the acropolis by means of a parallel battered support wall founded on trimmed bedrock ca. 1.50 m. south of the perimeter wall. Whatever its intended function may have been, numerous accumulated soil layers were found in the intervening space. Wall fragments, traces of *huwwar* surfaces, a door sill and storage pits indicated that additional domestic or public structures had occupied the space lying south of this support wall. The remains of this period, however, were partially disturbed by earthquake activity which was most apparent in Square D.3.

The complex accumulation of Early Roman remains on the south shelf of the *tell* gave us the clearest sequence of occupation history for the period. In Cave B.4:74 and in a "room" spanning the northern portion of Square B.4 and the southern portion of Square B.2 were series of soil layers which from both ceramic and coin evidence could be dated as Early Roman I (63-37 B.C.) occupation deposits. Smaller accumulations from the same period were found in Cave B.4:171. This domestic occupation came to an end by a major earthquake, probably the one recorded by other sources for 31 B.C., which caused the collapse of the ceiling of Cave B.4:171 so that it was never used for domestic purposes again, rendered Cave B.4:74 unusable except for a waste dump, and caused the redesign and repair of other living space in the Area.

During the Early Roman II-III period (37 B.C.-A.D. 73), according to the coin and ceramic evidence, the occupants of Esbus began an extensive redesign of the facilities on the south shelf. They constructed the first of a series of plastered surfaces over an extensive sector (running east-west for the greatest portion of the Area). It seems from the smoothness, thickness and physical composition of the layers tested, that the builders wanted to provide an adequate surface for extensive foot traffic, possibly leading to an access to the acropolis. An apparent stairway forming the south edge of this facility confirmed test results on some of the plaster samples in that the layers were of insufficient strength to support wheeled traffic of any size.[5] Whether this comprised a forum, plaza, roadway or market place was not clear to us.

In Area C the major structure from the Early Roman period was the large and well-built stone Wall C.1:40/63 set on bedrock in a foundation trench which followed roughly a scarp in the natural rock. The wall was 1.40 m. thick and survived to a height of over two meters. Its size as well as its placement suggested that it was part of the Early Roman defense system on the west side of the city.

Additional evidence of activity from this period was recovered in Cemetery F where Tomb F.18 had been cut and first used in the Early Roman period, as evidenced by six datable coins found in the tomb as well as by the pottery recovered from it.

*Late Roman* (A.D. 135-324). Late Roman remains on the acropolis included a substantial stone platform in Area A, Square 6, and three walls comprising the most impressive construction in

[5] Samples submitted to the laboratories of the Natural Resources Authority of Jordan were given preliminary analysis. An oral report of the results of these preliminary tests allowed this conclusion to be made before the 1973 season ended.

Square A.7. Both the platform and the walls had obviously been parts of public facilities, but the precise nature of their function was not learned. They indicated that a major structure had stood on the west side of the acropolis in Late Roman times.

During this period the south slope of the acropolis was drastically redesigned. After the destruction of what may have been a municipal or other public building, partially recovered in Square D.3, a monumental stone stairway leading up to the acropolis from the south was constructed. Portions of the stairs were recovered in spite of extensive robbing and later intrusions in both Squares D.3 and D.2. A coin found in the makeup materials for the stair construction had been issued by Trajan (A.D. 98-117), indicating that the stairs must have been laid during or after his reign. This monumental stairway seemed to connect the extensive plaster layers of Area B with any public structure that stood on the summit of the acropolis during this period.

The most significant find made in the layers of this period was a rare coin of Elagabalus (A.D. 218-222) minted at Esbus. The reverse bears the imprint "Esbous" underneath a four-columned temple facade and a statue of a deity or of the emperor in the center. The obverse shows the head of the emperor and the usual inscription surrounding it.

Evidence from the Late Roman period recovered in Area C was limited to some fill layers in pits. During this period Tomb F.12, discovered in the 1973 season, was cut from the rock and first used while Tomb F.18, constructed in the Early Roman period, was reused.

*Early Byzantine* (A.D. 324-491). The bulk of evidence from this period was recovered from the south slope and shelf of the *tell,* from the church on the acropolis, and from some tombs.

The chief feature of the Early Byzantine period found on the south slope was a water channel running north-south. This channel of which portions were recovered in Squares D.2 and D.3 was carefully covered with neatly fitted stones. In this period the

south exterior wall of the Christian church was constructed together with a catch basin and a drain to bring water, probably
from the roof, into the Cistern D.5:5 (excavated in 1971). Further
constructions carried out during this period included a staircase
over the water channel on the south slope and surfacings and
rooms south of the church inside the acropolis perimeter Wall
D.4:4, which continued as the main acropolis fortification. Cistern
D.6:33, constructed in Early Roman times, continued in use.

The evidence found in Area B showed that the plaster layers
leading to the stairway were repeatedly resurfaced during the
Early Byzantine period, although interruptions must have occurred, as an intrusive pit in Square D.4 and other evidence
showed.

Tomb F.18 was reused also in this period, while Tomb F.16
was cut in Early Byzantine times. It must have been used several
times, as indicated by the layered skeletal remains in one
chamber and the apparently single burial deposits in the other.

*Late Byzantine* (A.D. 491-640). The main evidence of this
period recovered was found on the acropolis and south slope, and
in the tombs. Inside the basilica two portions of mosaic floor
were discovered in the western extremity of its nave. The earlier
included a border pattern suggesting that it had been near
the end of the nave. It was bounded on the west by a Roman
wall still in use in Late Byzantine times. Above it lay a second
mosaic which seemed to continue westward through a possible
doorway. Tracing it toward the west was impossible because of
the balk and had to be postponed to a later season's work.

Outside the basilica on the north was a substantial room
comprised of reused Roman walls in which portions of a mosaic
floor of a mid-sixth century style survived. This confirmed
evidences discovered in previous seasons that the Byzantine
builders reused structural remains of the Roman period.

On the south side of the basilica a new water drain took the roof water into Cistern D.6:33, while new rooms and spaces were arranged south of the church.

Although no remains of the period survived in Area B on the south shelf, traces of a retaining wall were recovered in Square C.1 on the west shelf.

The Late Roman tomb F.12 was reused twice in the Late Byzantine period and several other tombs cleared in the 1973 season were first constructed and used (F.11a, F.11b, F.14 and F.17). Paritally cut, but apparently never used, was Tomb F.15.

*Umayyad* (A.D. 661-750). This season provided our first indisputably identifiable stratified Umayyad remains at *Tell Ḥesbân*. Dug down through the Byzantine floor in the room north of the basilica on the acropolis was a well-built *ṭabun* which seemed to have been built in the late 7th or 8th centuries. While evidence on the south slope of the *tell* was badly disturbed, the sector just inside the acropolis perimeter wall indicated that Cistern D.6:33 remained in use and that the surrounding surface remained partially intact. On the west slope only a pair of soil layers running up to a possible retaining wall (Square C.3) indicated settlement there during the Umayyad period. Though no tombs were found from this period, ceramic and soil stratification evidence suggested that some people must have opened Tomb F.18 in Umayyad times, but filled it after an inspection.

*'Abbāsid* (A.D. 750-969). Improved ceramic distinctions were made possible by the recovery of an isolated stratified 'Abbāsid construction for the first time at *Tell Ḥesbân*. While some sherds from the period had been identified in dump layers in Square C.2 on the west shelf and in a pit on the south shelf (Square D.4), it was a stone-lined pit with its foundation trench and interior soil layer (Square B.6) which allowed the recovery of a small group of homogeneous 'Abbāsid pottery for the first time in the series of seasons conducted thus far. This represented another step in the establishment of an increasingly refined ceramic horizon for East Jordan.

Following this occupation *Tell Ḥesbân* was apparently abandoned until the early stages of Late Islamic civilization revived the use of this site with major new construction activities over the existing ruins.

*Ayyūbid-Mamlūk* (A.D. 1174-1516). Extensive remains of this period found in previous seasons were further clarified by the 1973 excavations. Portions of the vaulted room just inside the south perimeter wall of the acropolis were recovered in Areas A (balk removal in Squares A.3 and 4) and D (Square D.6). Additional traces of similarly constructed rooms were found in Square A.6. Indicative of the sizable settlement in this period was the extensive bath installation overlying the west portion of the Byzantine basilica. It reused portions of both the earlier Byzantine and Roman structures along the western edge of the acropolis. This bathing complex consisted of a small entrance corridor which led into the bathing room that had a heated stone floor and a stone basin into which hot and cold water was led by separate pipes from two water tanks in the next room. The hot water tank rested on a brick-lined firing chamber which was fed from the stoker's room. The excavation of this bathing facility consumed much time, and since the Department of Antiquities wanted to preserve this installation it was impossible to ascertain the nature of the underlying remains of the church, or find its possible western terminus in this sector.

West of the bathing installation a narrow corridor between two long walls with a series of earth floors suggested the existence of additional commercial or domestic structures along the west perimeter wall of the acropolis.

On the south slope of the acropolis extensive pits outside the perimeter wall (D.4:4—now used in a fourth and final stage of its function as an acropolis boundary) indicated in conjunction with building remains three stages of occupation. The pits appeared to have been created by robbing earlier stone for construction purposes. Traces of Ayyūbid-Mamlūk occupation were also found in the other Areas and surroundings, but none were important enough to warrant detailed description in this summary.

Evidence that the occupants of *Tell Ḥesbân* had opened, then filled and resealed, tombs occurred in two instances (Tombs F.14 and F.18).

A probe was made outside and inside the south wall of the ruin of a large building standing in the present village. The evidence of stratification, ceramics and one Ayyūbid coin (Al-'Adil, A.D. 1196-1218) suggested that the construction of this building had taken place during the Ayyūbid-Mamlūk period.

The activities of the Survey team resulted in tracing the route of the Roman road leading from Livias in the Jordan valley toward Esbus. A major portion of this road was located. It brought the known route to about a kilometer from the *tell*, where traces disappeared and allowed at least three options for connections north, east or south. The evidence included milestones, curbing stones, portions of sub-surface roadbeds, foundations of guard-towers and road stations as well as ceramic samples gathered from ground surface soil.

Equally important were the results of the Survey team's effort to locate and collect pottery from the ground surface of 103 sites lying within a radius of ten kilometers of *Tell Ḥesbân*. This was the beginning of what can become an extended portrait of the density and nature of regional settlement to which the occupants of *Tell Ḥesbân* were economically, politically, and perhaps militarily related during the various cultural periods involved.

At the close of the 1973 season several major and some minor unsolved problems remained. Chief among these questions were the following: Where and what was the nature of the western terminus of the basilica? Were the cement floor in Square B.1 and the plastered retaining wall in Squares B.2 and B.4 parts of a constructed water reservoir? If not, what were they? Was the major Early Roman stone wall in Square C.1 part of the western defense installations? Were the substantial Iron II masonry remains in Square C.3 also defensive in function? Were the newly found indications of an occupation of the *tell* in the Iron I period indicative of a relatively minor settlement, or simply the accidentally minor clues of a more extensive occupation? Could gaps still existing in our knowledge of Heshbon's history possibly be closed by a more refined analysis of all data already recovered, or only by further excavations in sectors of *Tell Hesbân* not yet touched by our tools? These unanswered questions clearly showed that our task at ancient Heshbon was not yet complete.

# AREA A

BASTIAAN VAN ELDEREN
Calvin Theological Seminary, Grand Rapids, Michigan

During the 1968 and 1971 seasons six Squares were excavated in Area A, all but one (A.6) to bedrock.[1] Approximately three-fourths of a Byzantine church was uncovered—the apse, north aisle, south aisle, and nave, though its western end, with narthex and main entrance, was not located.

Also identified were traces of Islamic occupation—including water channels to feed cisterns below the church, a quarry north of the church, and northeast of the church a large cave containing evidence of Roman occupation.

The major objective of the 1973 season was to complete the excavation of the church—to expose the narthex and western wall containing the main entrance. A second objective was to finish excavating Square 6 to bedrock, and to integrate Areas A and D. The first objective was not fully accomplished because an extensive Islamic installation was encountered in the higher accumulation of debris along the western edge of the acropolis. Regarding the second objective, Square 6 was excavated to bedrock and Areas A and D were integrated.

*Square 7*—This square (6 x 8 m.) lay west of Square 5 and south of the east-west axis. Some exposed traces of architecture suggested that the ground surface of the acropolis, rising sharply along the western edge, contained the ruins of perimeter structures. This was conclusively demonstrated by the excavation of the new Square. (See Figure 2.)

The removal of the ground surface debris exposed two major north-south walls (A.7:2 and A.7:3) running roughly parallel. Wall A.7:2 (6.5 m. long and .80 m. wide) ran along and at a slight angle to the west balk so that its southern end was

[1] Bastiaan Van Elderen, "Heshbon 1968: Area A," *AUSS*, 7 (1969): 142-165; Dorothea Harvey, "Heshbon 1971: Area A," *AUSS*, 11 (1973): 17-34.

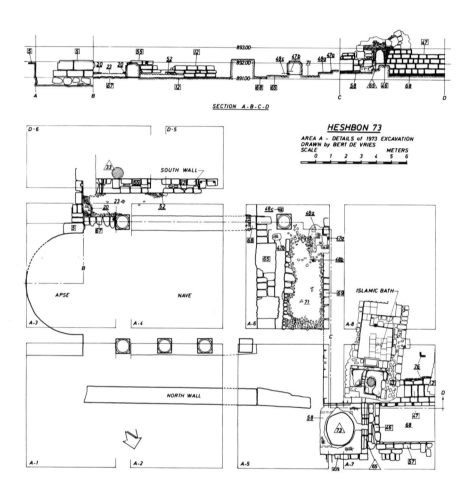

Fig. 2. Plan of excavated features in the western (Squares A. 5-8) and southeastern parts of Area A (Squares A.3-4 and D.5-6).

partially hidden in the balk. The east face of this wall was completely exposed to its founding level—five courses preserved in the northern part and eight courses in the southern part. About half of this wall was removed to expose features underneath.

Wall A.7:3 (6.25 m. long and .75 m. wide) lay across the middle of the Square. The northern half of this wall, where it curved towards Wall A.7:2, was removed to expose features underneath. A bath complex, built against the east face of the southern half (see below), was uncovered.

The sector between Walls A.7:2 and A.7:3, possibly a hallway or alley between two buildings, contained a number of beaten earth surfaces, all containing Ayyūbid/Mamlūk sherds. There were no doorways or windows opening into this passageway, except one doorway between the walls at the south end, near the south balk, which was used with only one of the surfaces. The removal of Wall A.7:2 revealed walls with plastered surfaces running to the west of it and perpendicular to it suggesting a complex of rooms.

*Islamic Bath*— The major architectural feature in Square 7 was an Islamic bath installation of the Ayyūbid/Mamlūk period in the southeast quarter of the Square. (See Fig. 3.) Evidence of this began appearing as soon as the ground surface debris was removed. The first parts to be exposed were two hemispherical tanks plastered inside (occupying a space of about 2 x 3 m.). The larger tank, for hot water, had been plastered at least five times. Both tanks drained into a stone basin (.99 x .54 m. and .22 m. deep) in the next room to the south (Pl. III:B). The basin had a drain on its south side which had been broken out. This room (2.50 x 2.20 m.) had a floor of large, smooth stone tiles, and walls with partially preserved plaster. Since the south wall lay outside of Square 7, a 4 x 2 m. extension was excavated to the south— Square 8.

This excavation of Square 8 revealed the south wall (A.8:2) of the bathing room with a doorway in the east end leading to an entrance hallway (2.25 x .85 m.) running east-west, with the same type of tile floor (A.8:7), partially destroyed. In the west end of the south wall of the hallway (A.8:5) was an entrance (A.8:6) which was .55 m. wide and plastered on the inside edges (suggesting a passageway rather than a door). Sizable portions of the plaster on the walls in the hallway and bathing room were preserved. In the west end of the hallway was a small plastered bench (A.8:9). The cleaning of Wall A.8:2 revealed a flue or chimney (A.8:10) which connected with the heating system below the entire bath complex (Pl. III:A).

In excavating the space north of the wall against which the water tanks were built, an opening with a three-course brick arch was found (Pl. II:A). This oval-shaped firebox (A.8:24) heated the water in the larger tank. It also heated the bathing room by means of a hypocaust-like heating chamber leading from the firebox and widening out under almost the whole floor of the room (Pl. II:B). In this the hot air circulated between small stone pillars that supported the basalt slabs on which the tile floor was laid. This hot-air chamber was filled with dirt and debris—with ash layers on the bottom.

North of the furnace was a room which appeared to be the "furnace room," of the Ayyūbid/Mamlūk period, like the rest of the installation. In it were found various layers of ash mixed with patches of *huwwar*. (See Fig. 3.)

Partly under and west of the furnace room was found an earlier room bounded by the north-south Wall A.7:46, and the east-west Walls A.7:57 and 7:47, the wide wall upon which the north side of the bath installation rested. (The west wall, lying apparently beyond the limits of Square 7, remained unexcavated.) Evidence from the foundation trenches of these three walls indicated a late Roman date.

To the east of this room appeared the fragment of a mosaic floor (A.7:58) which consisted of three rows of white tesserae laid along the walls and a field of white tesserae laid diagonally

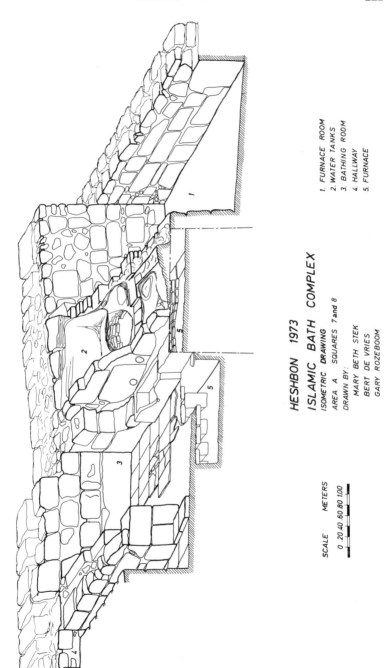

HESHBON   1973
ISLAMIC   BATH   COMPLEX

ISOMETRIC  DRAWING
AREA  A    SQUARES  7 and 8
DRAWN BY:
        MARY  BETH  STEK
        BERT  DE  VRIES
        GARY  ROZEBOOM

1. FURNACE  ROOM
2. WATER  TANKS
3. BATHING  ROOM
4. HALLWAY
5. FURNACE

SCALE      METERS
0  20 40 60 80 100

Fig. 3. An isometric drawing of the Islamic Bath complex as far as it was excavated in 1973.

(later it was discovered that this section of diagonally-laid tesserae was the surround of the design in the mosaic floor of a
room extending eastward). This will be dealt with after further
discussion of the westward-extending room.

An interesting phenomenon on the east side of north-south
Wall A.7:46 was a narrow channel (A.7:65) built against and
along its east face. It ran from Wall A.7:47 (from the hearth stone
or threshold [A.7:39] of the firebox) and up to Wall A.7:60,
clearly suggesting that the channel, associated with a Late Roman
wall, was part of an installation antedating the mosaic floor
(A.7:58).

These Late Roman walls gave rise to speculation about the
nature of this architecture, especially the east-west Wall A.7:47.
An impressive piece of construction, 1.50 m. wide, with well cut
and tightly fitted stone blocks, it continued eastward into the
balk between Squares 5 and 7, and part of its south face lay under
the Islamic bath installation. This major wall was re-used in the
Byzantine period: Mosaics A.7:58 and A.7:76 were laid up to it
on the north and south face respectively. Although the alignment
is not perfectly true, it seems possible that this major Wall A.7:47
was used as a continuation of the north wall of the Byzantine
basilica at its western end. This wall was partly re-used later in
the building of the bath installation, the then remaining top
course serving as the threshold for the arched entryway of the
firebox, and across it was built Wall A.7:3, which served as the
west wall of the bath installation. North of this wide wall a
hard-packed black earth surface (A.7:69), identified as Late
Roman also, extended to Wall A.7:57 west of Wall A.7:46. Two
unexcavated surfaces below this black floor (Surface A.7:78 and
*huwwar* Layer A.7:80), cut through by the foundation trenches of
Walls A.7:46, 47, and 57, were examined by a probe trench and
yielded Early Roman, Hellenistic, and Iron II (Persian period)
sherds.

No conclusive evidence of re-use of this western room in the

Byzantine period was found, although Byzantine sherds appeared mixed with Islamic sherds, and a small segment of mosaic was found in the southeast corner. A partly damaged wall (Wall A.7:70) to be associated with the Umayyad Surface A.7:68 was found in the west portion of the room. This sector became part of the "Furnace Room" for the Islamic bath installation after Wall A.7:3 had been cut through it to form the west wall.

As Mosaic A.7:58 was being exposed, east of Wall A.7:46 dividing it from the western room, it was noted that the center portion had been destroyed by a *tabun* (A.7:73), which was completely uncovered by the removal of the balk between Squares 5 and 7. This also revealed that the white tesserae of this mosaic formed the surround of a colored geometric design of the mosaic uncovered in the west edge of Square 5 (Pl. I:B). The Byzantine date for the use of this floor is indicated by the sherds found on it; and the similarity, in design and workmanship, to other more precisely dated mosaics in the Madeba region suggests a mid-sixth century date. This room, whose west, north, and south walls were identified, had apparently lost its east wall in subsequent construction. It was apparently an anteroom outside the basilica proper along its north wall, a type common in Byzantine churches.

The large *tabun* (A.7:73), whose construction had destroyed the central portion of the Mosaic A.7:58, had a long diameter of 2.00 m. for its outer rim. The upper layers of the destruction debris in the *tabun* contained Ayyūbid/Mamlūk sherds but inside this oven only Umayyad evidence was found, suggesting that it was built into the Byzantine floor in the seventh or eighth century.

In the southwest corner of Square 7, significant Byzantine evidence was found below the Islamic levels in the "passageway" between Walls A.7:2 and A.7:3, described above. A striking feature of the south face of Wall A.7:47, near the west balk, was a corner with the cross-wall only .08-.10 m. long. This wall stub appeared to be a door jamb. The removal of wall fragments and a beaten earth surface, all Umayyad, exposed a fragment of a Byzantine mosaic floor (A.7:76). The tesserae, laid diagonally, and slightly larger than those of Mosaic A.7:58, were white except for a few scattered colored ones used for repair work. This floor, laid up to the south face of Wall A.7:47, had a border of three rows of tesserae running parallel to the wall then around the above-mentioned door jamb and into the doorway. The corresponding southern door jamb was located by a similar border design. This mosaic floor continued into the south and west balks and under Wall A.7:3, the west wall of the bath installation. Hence the size and function of this room were not known. However, the doorway or passage identified was aligned with the north aisle of the basilica. Although the west edge of the doorway still lies in the balk, the continuation of the mosaic into the doorway (no threshold was found) suggested the presence of another room, perhaps the narthex of the church. Mosaic floors with white tesserae, found in both early and late Byzantine structures, frequently serve a utilitarian rather than a decorative function in rooms and spaces outside the main parts of the church.

*Square 6.*—In Square 6, opened in 1971, was found an Ayyūbid/ Mamlūk structure, possibly a house, built over the ruined Byzantine church. Evidences of the church included a column base (A.6:38) with a fragment of mosaic (A.6:37) attached on its west side, and a mosaic fragment (A.6:35) laid up to one of two paving stones (A.6:36) in the west balk.[2]

Between the 1971 and 1973 seasons, portions of the balks, especially the west balk of Square 6, had eroded extensively. Large stones, dislodged from the balk, partially destroyed its face. The 1973 objectives in Square 6 were to delineate the Byzantine and earlier occupation, and to continue the excavation to bedrock.

[2] D. Harvey, "Heshbon 1971: Area A," pp. 18-21.

North and east of Walls A.6:5 and A.6:6, the north and east walls of the Ayyūbid/Mamlūk house, was a crudely constructed kind of platform, consisting of column bases and column fragments. These large architectural members were removed along with Walls A.6:2, 5, and 6, in order to reach the layers underneath.

The removal of a gray-brown dirt layer (A.6:46) along the west balk exposed more mosaic (A.6:47) similar to A.6:35, which ran up to the east and north sides of the same two paving stones A.6:36; also other fragments of this floor south of Column Base A.6:38 and in the center of the Square. About ten centimeters below this mosaic near the west balk, a second mosaic (A.6:48) was found. This lower flooring was laid up to the paving stones (A.6:36) with a three-row border that also continued to the north, indicating the western edge of the mosaic.

The construction of the mosaics at *Tell Ḥesbân* is similar to that in other Byzantine mosaics: a foundation of small stones, a filler around the stones (brown clay), and over this foundation a cement underlayer in which the tesserae were set. Both foundations of these mosaics were fairly extensive in the Square. The absence of any mosaic fragments between the two mosaic foundation layers indicated that before the upper mosaic (A.6:47) was laid the lower one (A.6:48) was almost completely destroyed or removed. Three portions of this lower mosaic were preserved: one (described above) near the west balk, another near the northeast corner of Column Base A.6:38, and a third in the center of the Square.

Column Base A.6:38 was apparently raised to a level .18 m. higher than the other column bases found *in situ* in the basilica, but still in proper alignment with and spacing from the other column bases. This raising was done after the two building phases of the Byzantine church represented by the two mosaic floors (since both mosaic foundations are broken from the column base). Possibly this occurred when the base was replaced after dislocation caused by the destruction of the Byzantine church.

Accordingly, it seems that tesserae of Mosaic A.6:37 attached to the column base must be considered part of the fragments of the lower mosaic (A.6:48).

As described above, the border of the lower mosaic identifies its western edge along the west balk. This suggests the existence of a wall along the western edge of the mosaic, preserved in A.6:36 (identified as "paving stones" in 1971) and in Wall A.6:69, a north-south wall along the west balk of which the west half is in the balk.[3] This may have been the western wall of the nave of the first phase of the Byzantine church, which was at least partially removed in the second phase (an enlargement?) represented by the upper mosaic (A.6:47).

The lower mosaic (A.6:48) was attached to the western wall by three rows of tesserae running parallel to the wall. Between this and the field of the mosaic was a .35 m. surround of white tesserae laid diagonally. The field was surrounded by a border of colored tesserae with an entwining rope design. This border continued south beyond the westward extension of the line of the south row of column bases. This strongly suggested that this row of columns did not extend farther west, at least in the first phase of the church. If it had, there would be intercolumnar mosaic panels, not a border crossing the row. Excavation to the west could possibly reveal changes made in the second construction phase, but the 1973 evidence pointed to the existence of a west wall near the west balk.

In the southeast corner of the Square, between Column Base A.6:38 and the east balk, an Ayyūbid/Mamlūk surface was identified together with a narrow wall (A.6:40) along the east balk. Below this surface and wall was found the stone foundation layer (A.6:58) for the upper mosaic (A.6:47). The stone foundation layer (A.6:61) of the lower mosaic (A.6:48) was also identified in this sector. Directly below this, along the east side of and

___

[3] Although the foundation stones (A.6:61) of Mosaic A.6:48 did not run directly to this wall, the filler and cement underlayer did, indicating rather conclusively that the Mosaic A.6:48 also did.

below the Column Base A.6:38, there was found the un-robbed part of a well-built Early Roman north-south wall (A.6:65) running through the entire Square. This wall, laid in header-stretcher construction upon bedrock (the uneven surface was leveled by a layer of black plaster), had been shaved down when the first phase of the church was constructed. Further robbing apparently occurred when the second phase was constructed since the stone foundation layer (A.6:61) for the lower mosaic extended over the wall at its higher levels near the column base, but not in the sector in the middle of the Square where the surface of the wall had been lowered by robbing thus disturbing the stone foundation layer of the mosaic.

The stylobate wall supporting the south row of column bases was identified in Square 4 and dated to the Roman period in the 1971 season.[4] This wall was uncovered in Square 6 (A.6:68) where it was built up to but not bonded into the Early Roman north-south Wall A.6:65. Its Roman date was further confirmed, but its relationship to Wall A.6:65 indicates that it was later than that wall.

The function of Wall A.6:65 could not be ascertained at this time. Its size and construction were impressive and similar to the major east-west wall (A.7:47) in Square 7. If these two were part of the same building complex, they would have formed a corner in Square 5. Very little evidence of this could be found, although more investigation was thought necessary. The removal of the Byzantine layers from the Square, especially in the northern half, revealed the extensive Roman occupation. In addition to the well-built wall (A.6:65) described above, there was a layer of large stones (A.6:71), apparently a cobble floor or platform, in the western half of the Square. Along its eastern edge was a retaining wall (A.6:72); on the western side it butted against Wall A.6:69. This space between this platform and Wall A.6:65,

[4] *Ibid.,* pp. 25, 26.

slightly less than a meter, was filled in the same period by a small wall (A.6:77).

The middle portion of Surface A.6:71 was removed from the platform, revealing a substantial fill (A.6:80) of large stones and dirt containing Late Roman sherds, placed on the bedrock. This suggested a similar date for Surface A.6:71; and for Wall A.6:69, which predated this surface or platform and was laid on bedrock, an Early Roman date (or possibly earlier).

Since an Early Roman surface (A.6:76) covered the foundation trench of the major wall (A.6:65), it was later than that wall; but the same surface was cut by the foundation trench of Wall A.6:68; therefore the latter, the stylobate wall, was later than the major Wall A.6:65.

Directly above the bedrock (in Surface A.6:85 and Soil Layer A.6:88) were found Hellenistic sherds also mixed with some from the 7th-6th century B.C.; but no architectural features earlier than the Early Roman period.

*Squares 3 and 4.*—Removing the upper part of the balk between Squares 3 and 4 made possible the integration of some loci in Squares 3 and 4 identified in 1968: A.3:7 = A.4:13; A.3:11 = A.4:14; A.3:65 = A.4:51. The exact function of this last locus— eight cut stones laid in two rows—could not be determined. This could have been part of the structure for the screen separating the nave from the presbytery, which would have been the portion of the first bay between the easternmost columns and the ends of the apse walls. Further, traces of border design were found in the mosaic fragment (A.4:8) discovered in 1968; likewise in the mosaic fragment laid against the screen foundation, between the easternmost column base (A.4:45) and the south end of the apse wall (A.3:5).

The south balk of Square 4, portions of which had eroded away since 1968, was removed in order to integrate A.4 and D. 6. Below the top soil an Ayyūbid/Mamlūk wall (A.4:47) was uncovered, which equaled A.3:24 and D.6:68. This wall formed part of a room with Walls D.6:2 and 3. Below the soil layers under this wall were found various parts of a mosaic floor, traces of which were attached to the south exterior wall (D.6:55) of the basilica. White tesserae were laid in at least 14 rows parallel to the south wall, then in a field laid diagonally. Apparently scattered in this field were red, blue, and yellow diamond-shaped designs (one example of which was found intact). A similar field and design were found in Mosaic A.6:47 between the Column Base A.6:38 and the south balk. However, the level of Mosaic A.4:52 (891.30-.35 m.) corresponds with the level of Mosaic A.4:48 (891.32-.39 m.), rather than with that of Mosaic A.4:47 (891.46 m.). However, integration of mosaic surfaces by levels must allow at least a margin of variation of .10 to .15 m., especially if the portions are some distances apart.

Mosaic Stone Foundation Layer A.4:23 was laid directly up to Column Base A.4:45, thereby showing a surface connecting the column base and the south exterior wall of the church. Traces of mosaic were found attached to this column base in the same way and at the same level as the mosaic attached to Column Base A.6:38.

Further removal of the south balk of Square 4 involved probing the foundation trenches of the Stylobate Wall A.4:12 and of the south exterior wall of the church. This work confirmed and refined the conclusions reached in 1971 regarding A.4:12. Two foundation trenches were found—an upper one for the upper course of the wall which contained Byzantine sherds and a lower one which contained Early Roman sherds. This confirmed the suggestion of the 1971 Report that the Byzantine builders had re-used the lower courses of the Roman Wall A.4:12 and added an upper course to complete the stylobate wall.

Near the bottom of the south exterior wall of the church a solid Early Roman layer was identified which had been cut through by the Foundation Trench A.4:62 containing Late Roman sherds. This suggested a Late Roman date for at least the lower courses

of the south wall. On the south side of this wall in Area D,
Byzantine material was found to the bottom of the wall. Possibly,
the entire south side of the wall was cleared and exposed by the
Byzantine builders.

With the removal of the south balk in Square 4, a similar
operation was carried on in Square 3 with corresponding results.
The east-west wall (A.4:47) in Square 4 which formed part of
an Ayyūbid/Mamlūk room with Walls D.6:2 and 3 continued in
Square 3 (A.3:24) and formed a corner with Wall D.6:3. The
removal of this wall (A.3:24) revealed two soil layers underneath
from the same period. Below these layers was found a layer .16 m.
deep of tesserae, dirt, and cement fragments dating from the Late
Byzantine period. Fragments of the mosaic floor (A.3:20) in this
part (the south aisle) of the church were found. A segment of
mosaic was found attached to the column base and, although
the tesserae were missing between the base and the south exterior
wall, the preservation of the stone foundation layer (and in some
places the cement underlayer) of the mosaic clearly demonstrated that these fragments in Square 3 were to be correlated
with the fragments in the south aisle in Square 4.

The east wall of the south aisle was positively identified through
the traces of mosaic attached to it. In the mosaic along the south
exterior wall was a basin formed of white tesserae, seven centimeters deep. Similar basins have been found in mosaic floors in
other churches, such as in Swafiyeh and Madeba.

During the 1968 and 1971 seasons the south sacristy along the
apse was identified. Access to this room was by a doorway from
the south aisle. During the latter part of the second phase of the
church construction this doorway was blocked by a secondary
wall built across it. Another unusual feature of this room was
that its north-south dimension was larger than the width of the
south aisle. Usually the south exterior wall of the church would
be continued as the south wall of the sacristy. This room had a
mosaic floor; and the portions of the border and surrounding field,

and the walls to which the mosaic ran, indicate the actual size of the room, although the entire sector on the southeast exterior of the church was built over in the early Islamic period.

A segment of mosaic (A.3:20W) consisting of three rows of white tesserae was found lying between the easternmost column base and the west end of the south wall of the apse. This was attached to the column base and joined three rows of white tesserae lying along the east side of the column base. This mosaic segment was laid up to an east-west row of stones which possibly functioned as the base for the screen on the south side of the presbytery. The construction of this mosaic was the same as elsewhere. The cement underlayer (A.3:68) was found in places above the foundation layer of small stones (A.3:69).

Excavation below the level of the mosaic floor exposed the stylobate wall (A.3:67) which continued to the west end of the south wall of the apse. Its continuation beyond the easternmost column base (A.4:45) confirmed the conclusion that it was originally a Roman wall re-used in the construction of the church. Although the foundation trench of this wall was considerably disturbed by rodents, it was evident that the lower two courses were dated to the Roman period. This wall was built on bedrock.

## Summary

The 1973 season was very fruitful in contributing new light on the Islamic, Byzantine, and Roman occupations of Area A and in identifying a Hellenistic occupation.

The two previous seasons had established the Islamic occupation of the acropolis. In the center of the Area water channels were found which fed into various cisterns cut into the bedrock. Along the southern side of the acropolis various Ayyūbid/Mamlūk structures were identified in Area D. In 1973 architectural remains of the same period were found along the western side of the acropolis, principally the bath installation uncovered in Squares 7 and 8. Exposed architectural features as well as walls partially excavated indicated that sizable portions of these Ayyūbid/

Mamlūk structures lay to the west of the excavated Squares.

In addition, a definite Ummayad installation was identified—the large *ṭabun* set down through the mosaic floor in Square 7.

The major Byzantine feature in Area A was the large Christian basilica, identified in 1968 when the apse and portions of the nave and side aisles were excavated together with some fragments of mosaic floors. In 1971 more of the apse and side aisles were uncovered. The 1973 excavations further clarified the existence of at least two phases of the Byzantine church when a mosaic floor was found superimposed on an earlier one in Square 6. There was some evidence that in the later phase the western end of the basilica was modified or enlarged by the removal of the western wall of the nave. The western exterior wall of the basilica in the second phase seemed to lie beyond the 1973 excavations in Square 7, as indicated by the mosaic floor found in the southwest corner of that Square. In addition, in this second phase there was at least one room outside the basilica proper on the north side. This room had a mosaic floor with geometric intertwining designs.

Antedating the Byzantine church was a major architectural feature on the western half of the acropolis, indicated by massive well-built Roman walls (in Squares 6 and 7), re-used in Square 7 by the Byzantine builders and in some cases again by the Islamic builders. The extent and identity of this Roman building awaits further excavation; the architecture clearly suggests some type of major public building.

Traces of Hellenistic and Iron Age occupation, found directly above the bedrock, were not adequate to identify any occupation features. Possibly the Roman builders cleared the acropolis in order to build the major structures on bedrock.

Questions remain to be answered in Area A: How extensive were the Islamic buildings on the western side of the acropolis? How large was the Byzantine church and what were its related structures? What were the prior Roman structures on the acropolis? Where there earlier occupation layers on the acropolis?

# AREA B AND SQUARE D.4

JAMES A. SAUER

American Center of Oriental Research
Amman, Jordan

In addition to the four Area B Squares of 1968 and 1971 (B.1, B.2, B.3, B.4),[1] three new Squares were worked in the Area in 1973 (B.5, B.6, D.4).[2] Square B.5 was a 2.00 x 2.00 m. probe north of B.2, and B.6 was a 1.00 x 6.00 m. probe west of B.1. Both were planned to test the lateral extent of the Strata 5-12 plaster layers. Square D.4 was laid out east of B.3, to link Area B with Area D. While Squares B.5 and B.6 were each worked only a few weeks, the other five Squares were excavated during most or all of the seven-week season. As part of the work in B.2, the balk between Squares B.2 and B.4 was taken down stratigraphically, and it is designated herein as Balk-B.2. In 1973 Area B continued to utilize the dump southeast of Square D.4.

## Ayyūbid/Mamlūk Strata 2-3 (ca. A.D. 1200-1456)

*1968, 1971:* In addition to the Modern remains of Stratum 1, Ayyūbid/Mamlūk remains of Strata 2 and 3 were attested in Area B in 1968 and 1971. The Stratum 2 ground surface soil covered Area B, and the Stratum 3 pits and robber trench cut down into the Early Byzantine ff. remains of Strata 4 ff., but no Ayyūbid/Mamlūk structures were attested in 1968 or 1971.

*1973 Description (Stratification):*[3] In addition to the Stratum 2 ground surface soil and the Stratum 3 pits, Ayyūbid/Mamlūk

---

[1] For the results of the 1968 season, cf. D. M. Beegle, "Heshbon 1968: Area B," *AUSS* 7 (1969) : 118-126; E. N. Lugenbeal and J. A. Sauer, "Seventh-Sixth Century B.C. Pottery from Area B at Heshbon," *AUSS* 10 (1972): 21-69. For the results of the 1971 season, cf. J. A. Sauer, "Heshbon 1971: Area B," *AUSS* 11 (1973) : 35-71; J. A. Sauer, *Heshbon Pottery 1971* (Berrien Springs, Mich., 1973) , pp. 1-74. While the present report regularly includes references to the results of the 1968 and 1971 seasons, it assumes prior familiarity with the above reports, especially with the descriptions and interpretations of "Heshbon 1971: Area B."

[2] Cf. Figs. 1, 4. Square D.4 was included in the Area D numbering sequence in 1971, but in 1973 it was excavated as part of Area B.

[3] Pre-excavation cleanup in Squares B.1-B.4 consisted of Loci B.1:117, B.2:71, B.3:49, and B.4:77,79,82. These Loci produced the following bones:

133

structures and associated soil layers were attested in Area B (Balk-B.2, B.5, B.6, D.4) in 1973.

The Stratum 2 ground surface soil (Balk-B.2:1; B.5:1, 2; B.6:1; D.4:1) partially covered the Ayyūbid/Mamlūk remains in the Area, and completely covered the 'Abbāsid and the Early Byzantine remains.

In Balk-B.2, the robber Trench B.2:18, 32 of Stratum 3 cut down into the Early Byzantine—Late Roman plaster layers of Strata 7-11 (B.2:15-31 a-d).

Beneath the Stratum 2 ground surface soil in Square B.5 were two superimposed plaster layers (B.5:3, 4) which rested on a soil layer (B.5:5) over a small-rock layer (B.5:6). The roughly horizontal plaster layers were thin (ca. .05-.20 m.) and badly eroded, while the soil and the small-rock layers were each quite thick (ca. .35-.70 m., and ca. .10-.25 m. respectively). These Ayyūbid/Mamlūk layers, which lay above the Early Byzantine Stratum 7 layers in the Square (B.5:7-10), had no Strata 2, 3 counterparts in B.1-4 in 1968 or 1971.

In B.6, two Ayyūbid/Mamlūk walls (B.6:11, 10) were set down into the Early Byzantine—Roman stratification (Strata 5-12) in the Square.

Wall B.6:11 ran north-south through B.6, ca. 3.00 m. west of the east balk of the Square, and its top surviving stones were visible in the unexcavated ground surface soil north and south of the Square. The wall was constructed of medium-sized (ca. .25-.40 m.) stones, and it was only one course thick. It was preserved to a height of only two courses. On the east side of the wall, its foundation trench (B.6:12) was dug down into the Square's Early Byzantine—Roman Strata 5-12 plaster layers (B.6:5, 4). On the

| Sheep/Goat | 102 | Horse | 1 | Domestic Chicken | 3 |
| Cattle | 4 | Large Mammal | 2 | Wild Bird | 1 |
| Donkey | 1 | | | | |

The cleanup Loci also produced the following registered artifacts:

| B.3:49 | 1521 | Coin (A.D. 138-161) | B.4:82 | 1453 | Slingstone |
| B.4:82 | 1321 | Iron Ring | B.4:82 | 1469 | Iron Clamp |
| B.4:82 | 1322 | Iron Hook | | | |

west, Layer B.6:13 sealed against the wall, and it covered over the
B.6:14, 15 foundation trench of the earlier (Ayyūbid/Mamlūk)
Wall B.6:10.

Wall B.6:10 also ran north-south through B.6, ca. 1.00 m.
west of Wall B.6:11. It was constructed of larger (ca. .40-.70 m.)
stones, and it was one course thick, but five courses of its western
face were exposed during excavation. On the east, the wall's
B.6:14, 15 foundation trench lay beneath Layer B.6:13 and Wall
B.6:11, and it had been cut down into the Early Byzantine—
Roman Strata 5-12 plaster layers. On the west, a ca. 1.00 m.
deep rock tumble layer (B.6:7) sealed against the wall, and this
layer rested on two superimposed plaster layers (B.6:8, 9).
Plaster Layer B.6:8 sealed against the wall, and plaster Layer
B.6:9 (exposed but not excavated) seemed to seal against it as
well.

In D.4, the Stratum 2 ground surface soil partially covered a
shallow Ayyūbid/Mamlūk wall (D.4:6) in the northwest corner
of the Square, as well as another shallow wall (D.4:5) in the
southwest corner of the Square. It also partially covered two
walls of a deeply founded Ayyūbid/Mamlūk structure (D.4:2,
13) in the southeast portion of the Square.

In the northwest corner of D.4, Wall D.4:6 ran eastward ca.
3.00 m. into the Square from the west balk, and its line was
visible in the unexcavated ground surface soil north of B.3 and
B.2. The wall was constructed of large (ca. .50-1.00 m.) roughly
squared stones, and it was two courses thick and survived one
course high. It rested in the D.4:1 Stratum 2 ground surface soil,
and it lay over the Early Byzantine Stratum 5 plaster Layer
D.4:3, and over the D.4:7, 8 'Abbāsid pit.

In the southwest corner of D.4, Wall D.4:5 ran ca. 2.00 m.
northwestward into the Square from the south, and its line was
also visible in the unexcavated ground surface soil south of D.4.
The wall was constructed of large (ca. .25-.75 m.) rectangular-

cut stones, and it was two courses thick and survived only one course high.

In the southeast portion of D.4, north-south Wall D.4:2 and east-west Wall D.4:13 formed the northwest bonded corner of a deeply founded Ayyūbid/Mamlūk structure. Both walls were constructed of large (ca. .40-.80 m.) roughly squared stones, and within the Square they both were ca. 2.00 m. long. The walls were preserved to a height of 9-10 courses, but they were "faced" only towards the interior of the structure. The exterior "faces" of the walls merged into the rock tumble of their foundation trenches (D.4:17 to the west of Wall D.4:2,[4] and D.4:10 to the north of Wall D.4:13). The D.4:17, 10 foundation trenches were cut through the Early Byzantine—Late Roman and earlier (Strata 6-10 ff.) layers in the Square (D.4:4 ff.), apparently to found the walls on bedrock (D.4:25, 26). Inside the structure, two rock tumble layers (D.4:12, 14), ca. 2.00 m. deep, covered over a soil layer (D.4:19=21) which sealed against the two walls, and which covered over cracked bedrock (D.4:25, 26). At the level of Bedrock D.4:25, 26, but in the south balk of the Square, Layer D.4:19=21 also covered over a possible vaulted "cellar" (D.4:24), which was exposed but not excavated in 1973.

*1973 Description (Bones):* The Ayyūbid/Mamlūk Loci produced the following bones in 1973:

| | | | | | | |
|---|---|---|---|---|---|---|
| Sheep/Goat | 119 | Large Mammal | 9 | Domestic Chicken | 8 |
| Cattle | 19 | Dog | 2 | Snail | 134 |
| Horse | 1 | Poss. Cat | 2 | Human | 16 |
| Donkey | 1 | Rodent | 1 | | |

It should be noted that Loci D.4:12, 14 produced all 16 of the disarticulated human bones, as well as 130 of the 134 snail shells.

*1973 Description (Artifacts):* The latest pottery from the above Loci was Ayyūbid/Mamlūk. A single 1382-1399 Mamlūk coin came from Locus D.4:1 (Object 1527). In addition, the following registered artifacts came from the Ayyūbid/Mamlūk Loci:[5]

---

[4] Loci D.4:15, 16 were shallow pits which spread out irregularly, for several meters, from the western edge of foundation Trench D.4:17. These Loci may have been part of D.4:17, or they may have been independent pits like those uncovered in B.4 in 1971 (Stratum 3).

[5] Only registered artifacts have been included in this report. Numerous other artifacts, especially of glass and of stone, were found and were saved, but were not registered as "objects."

| B.2:1 | 1465 | Glass Bead | D.4:1 | 1371 | Slingstone |
| B.2:18 | 1498 | Bronze Bracelet | D.4:12 | 1423 | Iron Hook |
| D.4:1 | 1326 | Copper Bracelet | D.4:12 | 1432 | Shell Bead |
| D.4:1 | 1330 | Iron Nail | D.4:12 | 1443 | Cloth Pouch |
| D.4:1 | 1347 | Perforated Clay Disk | D.4:17 | 1479 | Perforated Clay Disk |

*1973 Interpretation:* The new evidence for Ayyūbid/Mamlūk structures in Area B would agree with that from Areas A, C, and D, where extensive Ayyūbid/Mamlūk architectural remains were uncovered in 1968, 1971, and 1973. In addition to the Stratum 3 Ayyūbid/Mamlūk robbing and pitting, which was well attested in 1971, Ayyūbid/Mamlūk construction work would now be evident in Area B as well. Yet this construction would not seem to have been carried out according to a coherent plan in the Area excavated to date.

The B.5:3, 4 plaster layers did not have any counterparts in B.1-4, but these layers could possibly be compared to similar plaster layers in D.1 and D.2 which were associated with the Area D stairway/gateway (D.1:11, 23; D.1:17=D.2:10; D.2:8).

The B.6:11 wall would seem to have been a boundary wall, perhaps for agriculture, while the B.6:10 wall could have belonged to a domestic complex to the west. Since Wall B.6:11 postdated Wall B.6:10, there would be architectural evidence for two phases of Ayyūbid/Mamlūk activity in Square B.6.

In D.4, Walls D.4:6 and D.4:5 would also seem to have been late, shallow boundary walls.

In the southeast portion of D.4, the D.4:2, 13 structure could have been part of a domestic complex. However, since it was constructed below ground level, and since it contained disarticulated human bones, it could also have been part of a funerary installation.

Since most of the Ayyūbid/Mamlūk structures were constructed in, or were only partially covered by, the Stratum 2 ground surface soil, it would seem likely that they should be dated to the Mamlūk (ca. 1260-1456) rather than to the Ayyūbid (ca. 1200-1260) period, and the A.D. 1382-1399 Mamlūk coin from Locus D.4:1 would agree with this suggestion. The B.5:3-6 layers and the B.6:10 wall could perhaps be Ayyūbid in date. However, the evidence in Area B is not yet strong enough to allow for clear distinctions to be made between the Ayyūbid and the Mamlūk structural remains.

The absence of pig bones from the Ayyūbid/Mamlūk Loci should be noted here, since this evidence would agree with a Moslem occupation (cf. below, Early Byzantine).

### 'Abbāsid (ca. A.D. 750-878)

*1968, 1971:* No 'Abbāsid remains were attested in Area B in 1968 or 1971, since nothing was found in the Area between the Ayyūbid/Mamlūk remains of Strata 2 and 3, and the Early Byzantine remains of Stratum 4.

*1973 Description (Stratification):* Two 'Abbāsid pits, beneath the Ayyūbid/Mamlūk ground surface soil of Stratum 2, were found to be dug down into the Early Byzantine remains of Strata 4-7 in Area B in 1973.

In B.6, stone-lined Pit B.6:2 lay beneath the B.6:1 ground surface soil, ca. .40 m. west of the east balk. The pit had a diameter of ca. 1.25 m., and its two-course thick lining was constructed of small (ca. .10-.40 m.) stones. The pit's foundation Trench B.6:6 was dug down into the uppermost part of the B.6:5, 4 Early Byzantine—Roman plaster layers of Strata 5-12. No use surfaces were preserved against the pit exterior, but it did contain a layer of brown ashy soil (B.6:3).

In the north balk of D.4, Pit D.4:7, 8 lay beneath the Ayyūbid/Mamlūk D.4:1 ground surface soil and D.4:6 wall. The pit was dug down into the D.4:3, 4 ff. Early Byzantine plaster and soil layers of Strata 5-7, and it apparently intersected an Early Byzantine pit of Stratum 4 (D.4:9, 11) to the east. Pit D.4:7, 8 had a diameter of ca. 1.50 m., was ca. 1.25 m. deep, and contained soft black soil and small rocks.

*1973 Description (Bones):* The 'Abbāsid Loci produced the following bones in 1973:

Sheep/Goat    8            Cattle    5            Domestic Chicken    3

*1973 Description (Artifacts):* The latest pottery from the above Loci was 'Abbāsid. Pit B.6:2 produced an essentially homogeneous, if small, group of 'Abbāsid pottery, while the pottery from Pit D.4:7, 8 was very mixed. No coins were attested, but the following registered artifacts came from the 'Abbāsid Loci:

D.4:7    1374    Iron Spike            D.4:8    1403    Iron Nail
D.4:7    1383    Iron Spatula

*1973 Interpretation:* The new evidence for an 'Abbāsid occupation in Area B would agree with that from Area C, where 'Abbāsid traces were also found in 1973. No 'Abbāsid coins have yet come from the site, but an 'Abbāsid literary reference would indicate that *Hesbân* did not cease to exist in A.D. 750,[6] as had been suggested in 1971.[7]

The two pits in Area B would thus seem to reflect a minor use of the Area in the 'Abbāsid period, perhaps as a camping place.

The absence of pig bones from the 'Abbāsid Loci should again be noted here (cf. above, Ayyūbid/Mamlūk).

### Early Byzantine Strata 4-9 (ca. A.D. 324-410)

*1968, 1971:* Early Byzantine remains of Strata 4-9, covered over and cut into by the Ayyūbid/Mamlūk remains of Strata 2 and 3, were attested in Area B in 1968 and 1971. Stratum 4 consisted of Installation B.1:10 and Wall B.1:8B, both of which cut down into Strata 5ff. Strata 5, 7-9 were Area-wide super-imposed plaster and soil layers, while Stratum 6 was a rock tumble layer between Stratum 5 and Stratum 7. Early Byzantine Strata 5-9 continued the Area-wide plaster and soil layers of Late Roman Strata 10-11 and Early Roman Stratum 12. In the southwest corner of B.4, south of Wall B.4:46, several Early Byzantine layers (Stratum 9?) apparently sealed against and over Wall B.4:71 (partially exposed).

*1973 Description (Stratification):* Additional remains of Early Byzantine Strata 4-9 were attested in Area B (Balk-B.2, B.5, B.6, D.4) in 1973. The strata lay beneath and were cut into by the Ayyūbid/Mamlūk remains of Strata 2, 3, and they were also cut into by the 'Abbāsid pits.

[6] Cf. O. Grabar, "A Small Episode of Early 'Abbasid Times," *Eretz-Israel* 7 (1963): 44-47; W. Vyhmeister, "The History of Heshbon from Literary Sources," *AUSS* 6 (1968) : 171.

[7] Cf. "Heshbon 1971: Area B," 44.

Stratum 4 was represented in D.4 by Pit D.4:9, 11, a pit along the north balk of the Square which contained many small (ca. .02-.05 m.) rocks. The pit lay beneath Ayyūbid/Mamlūk ground surface Soil D.4:1, and it was apparently cut into by 'Abbāsid Pit D.4:7, 8. It was ca. .80 m. deep and ca. 2.00 m. wide east-west, and it was dug down into the D.4:4, 27, 18A Early Byzantine layers of Strata 6 and 7.

Stratum 5 was attested in the northwest corner of D.4, where the D.4:3A, 3B plaster and soil layers lay beneath Ayyūbid/ Mamlūk ground surface Soil D.4:1 and Wall D.4:6. The D.4:3 layers were cut by 'Abbāsid Pit D.4:7, 8 on the east, and they tapered into the ground surface soil towards the south. They covered over the Early Byzantine D.4:4, 20 rock tumble layer of Stratum 6.

Stratum 5 was also possibly attested in B.6. In the eastern portion of B.6, the B.6:5, 4 plaster layer lay under Ayyūbid/ Mamlūk ground surface Soil B.6:1, and it was cut into by the B.6:6 foundation trench of 'Abbāsid Pit B.6:2. Towards the west, it was cut off by the B.6:12 and B.6:14, 15 foundation trenches of Ayyūbid/Mamlūk Walls B.6:11 and B.6:10. The B.6:5, 4 layer, exposed but not excavated in 1973, was ca. 1.25 m. thick, and it was composed of many thin plaster layers. Since the uppermost level of B.6:5, 4 was ca. 887.75 m., and since the uppermost level of the B.1:6A (Stratum 7) plaster layer was ca. 887.50 m., it would seem likely that the upper .25 m. of the B.6:5, 4 layer belonged to Stratum 5. The lower 1.00 m. of the layer would correspond to Early Byzantine Strata 7-9, Late Roman Strata 10-11, and Early Roman Stratum 12.

Stratum 6 was represented in D.4 by the D.4:4, 20 rock tumble layer, which lay beneath the D.4:3 layers of Stratum 5. In the southeast portion of D.4, the rock tumble layer was cut through by the D.4:17, 10 foundation trenches of the D.4:2, 13 Ayyūbid/ Mamlūk structure. In the northern portion of the Square, it was also cut through by 'Abbāsid Pit D.4:7, 8 and Early Byzantine

Pit D.4:9, 11 (Stratum 4). The layer contained many large (ca. .25-.60 m.) rocks in the northeast portion of the Square, but towards the east and the south there were fewer and smaller rocks. The layer rested on top of the D.4:22, 23, 27 plaster layer of Stratum 7.

Stratum 7 was attested in Balk-B.2 and in D.4, and also probably in B.6. It may also have been present in Square B.5.

In Balk-B.2, beneath ground surface Soil B.2:1, the B.2:15, 17 plaster layer lay over the B.2:19 soil layer, and both of these layers were cut into by the B.2:18, 32 Ayyūbid/Mamlūk robber trench of Stratum 3. The plaster and soil layers rested above the B.2:20 plaster layer of Stratum 8.

In D.4, the D.4:22, 23, 27 plaster layer, beneath the rock tumble layer of Stratum 6, lay over the D.4:18a soil layer. The plaster and soil layers both sloped up evenly eastward, but the plaster layer became less distinct in that direction. The layers were cut by the D.4:2, 13 Ayyūbid/Mamlūk structure, the D.4:7, 8 ʿAbbāsid pit, and the D.4:9, 11 Early Byzantine pit of Stratum 4. They lay over the D.4:18b plaster layer of Stratum 8.

In B.6, the ca. 1.25 m. thick B.6:5, 4 plaster layer, unexcavated, would probably include Stratum 7 (cf. above, Stratum 5). The layer was cut off to the west by the foundation trenches of Ayyūbid/Mamlūk Walls B.6:11, 10.

In B.5, Stratum 7 may possibly have been represented by the B.5:7-10 plaster and soil layers (partially excavated), which lay beneath the B.5:1-6 Ayyūbid/Mamlūk remains in the Square. The combined layers were ca. .60-1.15 m. deep, but they were very uneven within the Square. The uppermost level of Layer B.5:7 varied from ca. 887.75 m. to ca. 888.40 m.

Like Stratum 7, Strata 8 and 9 were attested in Balk B.2, in D.4, and probably in B.6. In Balk-B.2, Stratum 8 consisted of plaster Layer B.2:20 over soil Layer B.2:21, and in D.4 the stratum consisted of plaster Layer D.4:18b over soil Layer D.4:28a. Stratum 9 lay beneath Stratum 8, and in Balk-B.2 it consisted of plaster Layer B.2:22 over soil Layer B.2:23, and in D.4 it consisted of plaster Layer D.4:28b=29 over soil Layer D.4:28c, 30. In B.6, Strata 8 and 9 would probably be included in the unexcavated B.6:5, 4 plaster layer (cf. above, Stratum 5). Strata 8 and 9 were cut by the Ayyūbid/Mamlūk B.2:18, 32 robber trench, D.4:2, 13 walls, and B.6:11, 10 walls. In D.4, Stratum 9 covered over the D.4:34 Late Roman rock tumble (from Wall D.4:32), as well as Wall D.4:31 and Locus D.4:30a, while elsewhere it rested on top of the Late Roman plaster layer of Stratum 10.

*1973 Description (Soil Samples):*[8] Soil samples were taken from the red clay lining in the B.1:10 installation of Stratum 4, and from the white material in the B.1:71 plaster layer of Stratum 5 (both excavated in 1971).

*1973 Description (Bones):* The Early Byzantine Loci of Strata 4-9 produced the following bones in 1973:

| Sheep/Goat | 293 | Poss. Calf | 1 | Domestic Chicken | 6 |
|---|---|---|---|---|---|
| Cattle | 36 | Large Mammal | 3 | Snail | 4 |
| Poss. Horse | 4 | Pig | 15 | Human | 1 |
| Poss. Donkey | 1 | Small Mammal | 2 | | |

It should be noted that the single human bone came from Pit D.4:9, 11.

*1973 Description (Artifacts):* The latest pottery from the above Loci was Early Byzantine, and a ca. A.D. 4th century coin came from Locus B.5:8 (Object 1539).[9] In addition, the Early Byzantine Loci produced the following registered artifacts:

| D.4:4 | 1398 | Bronze Buckle | D.4:4 | 1466 | Faience Bead |
|---|---|---|---|---|---|
| D.4:4 | 1436 | Iron Nail | D.4:18A | 1490 | Lead Weight |
| D.4:4 | 1442 | Bone Dice | D.4:18A | 1511 | Bone Needle |
| D.4:4 | 1458 | Small Iron Hook | D.4:28A | 1611 | Inscribed Base |

*1973 Interpretation:* The interpretations which were suggested for Early Byzantine Strata 4-9 in 1971 would seem to be supported by the new 1973 evidence.

Since Pit D.4:9, 11 cut down into Strata 5-7, it could probably be associated with Kiln B.1:10 of Stratum 4. Kiln B.1:10 cut down into Strata 5-12, and it would seem to reflect a radical restructuring of Area B (and the acropolis) in the early 5th century A.D.

[8] Only soil samples which have been submitted for analysis have been included in this report. Other samples (organic, mineral, soil) were taken in 1973, but analysis is not yet completed.

[9] Note also the A.D. 2nd-4th century coin (Object 1538) which was found during cleanup of Locus B.2:80 (cf. below, n. 20).

The Strata 5, 7-9 plaster and soil layers could still be interpreted as roadway resurfacings. They were attested from B.6 in the west to D.4 in the east, for a total length of ca. 35 m. They were also apparently attested from B.5 in the north to B.4 in the south, for a total width of ca. 19 m. In the west, they were cut off by the foundation trenches of Ayyūbid/Mamlūk Walls B.6: 11, 10, and originally they could have extended farther west, or they could have been retained there by a robbed out wall. In the east, they continued faintly into the east balk of D.4, and they covered Wall D.4:32, which retained the Stratum 10 Late Roman layer (cf. below). In the north, the layers were uneven in B.5, but they seemed to continue through that small Square to the north. In the south, the layers sloped down over partially robbed out Wall B.4:46, which originally would have retained the Strata 10-12 Roman layers (cf. below), as well as over the B.4:71, 155, 156 "stairway" of Strata 10-12 (cf. below). The layers sloped up eastward through Area B, and they could still probably be associated with the Area D. stairway/gateway. Because of their width, they could perhaps be termed a "plaza" as much as a "roadway," but they would still seem to reflect the history of the two Roman roads which met at Ḥesbân. The coin from B.5:8 would agree with the ca. A.D. 324-400 date which was suggested in 1971 for Strata 5-9.

The Stratum 6 rock tumble layer could still be interpreted in the context of the A.D. 365 earthquake.

The pig bones from Early Byzantine Strata 4-9 should be noted here, since they would contrast with the Ayyūbid/Mamlūk and the 'Abbāsid bone evidence (cf. above). They could be expected in either a pagan or a Christian context.

### Late Roman Strata 10-11 (ca. A.D. 135-324)

*1968, 1971:* Late Roman remains of Strata 10 and 11, cut into by Ayyūbid/ Mamlūk Stratum 3 and by Early Byzantine Stratum 4, lay beneath and were cut into by Early Byzantine Stratum 9. Strata 10 and 11 were primarily Area-wide plaster and soil layers, and they would probably have been retained on the south by east-west Wall B.4:46, which was partially robbed out by Early

Byzantine Stratum 9. These Late Roman layers continued the Area-wide plaster and soil layers of Early Roman Stratum 12.

*1973 Description (Stratification):* A new Late Roman rock tumble layer (D.4:34, 36) was attested in D.4 in 1973, and additional remains of the Strata 10 and 11 plaster layers were attested in Balk-B.2, in D.4, and probably in B.6. In the southern portion of B.4 and in the northeast corner of D.4, additional Late Roman remains were attested which lay outside the portion covered by the Strata 10 and 11 plaster layers. The Area B Late Roman remains lay beneath Early Byzantine Stratum 9, and they were cut into by the Ayyūbid/Mamlūk foundation trenches and Stratum 3 pits.

The D.4:34, 36 rock tumble layer lay beneath the D.4:28c, 30 Early Byzantine soil layer of Stratum 9, and it lay on top of the D.4:35 plaster layer and D.4:37 soil layer of Late Roman Stratum 10. The layer was ca. 1.00 m. deep, and in addition to its large (ca. .25-.70 m.) rocks (D.4:34), it contained pockets of red ashy soil (D.4:36). The tumble lay against the west "face" of Wall D.4:32, which ran north-south into the Square ca. 2.00 m. west of the east balk. While Wall D.4:32 had no preserved face on the west, it had a face surviving two courses high of finely squared stones on the east. Both the D.4:34, 36 rock tumble layer and the D.4:32 wall were cut off to the south by the D.4:10 foundation trench of the D.4:2, 13 Ayyūbid/Mamlūk structure.

The Stratum 10 plaster and soil layers were attested in Balk-B.2, in D.4, and probably in B.6. In Balk-B.2, the stratum consisted of plaster Layers B.2:24a-d over soil Layer B.2:27, and in D.4 it included plaster Layer D.4:35 (exposed but not excavated) over soil Layer D.4:37 (partially excavated, over unexcavated D.4:38). In D.4, the Stratum 10 layers also sealed against the west "face" of Wall D.4:32, beneath the D.4:34, 36 rock tumble layer. In B.6, the B.6:5, 4 plaster layer would probably include Stratum 10 (cf. above, Early Byzantine Stratum 5). The Stratum 10 layers were cut into by Ayyūbid/Mamlūk Loci B.2:18, 32, D.4:2, 13, and B.6:11, 10.

Stratum 11 was attested in Balk-B.2, and probably in B.6. In Balk-B.2, the thin B.2:31a-d plaster layers lay beneath the B.2:27 soil layer of Stratum 10, and they continued the thin B.2:31e-h plaster layers of Early Roman Stratum 12. In B.6, the B.6:5, 4 plaster layer would again probably include Stratum 11 (cf. above, Early Byzantine Stratum 5). Like Stratum 10, the Stratum 11 layers were cut into by Ayyūbid/Mamlūk Loci B.2:18, 32, D.4:2, 13, and B.6:11, 10.

In the southwest corner of B.4, beneath Early Byzantine Stratum 9, Layer B.4:129 sealed against the south face of Wall B.4:46, as well as against the west face of Wall B.4:71. Wall B.4:71 was the westernmost wall of the B.4:71, 155, 156 "stairway," which butted up against the south face of Wall B.4:46, and which stepped down from the west to the east (cf. below, Early Roman Stratum 12). In the southeast corner of B.4, red Layers B.4:112, 113, 119 sealed against the south face of Wall B.4:46, as well as against the east face of Wall B.4:156 (the easternmost wall of the "stairway"), and they continued over Bedrock B.4:193 into the east and south balks of the Square.[10] These layers lay beneath Ayyūbid/Mamlūk "Pit" B.4:33=40 of Stratum 3.

In northeastern D.4, the Early Byzantine Layer D.4:28c, 30 covered over Wall D.4:31 and Locus D.4:30a, as well as Wall D.4:32. Wall D.4:31 was an east-west wall surviving two courses high, which appeared in the north balk of D.4. It was constructed of large (ca. .40-.80 m.) roughly squared stones, and at the balk line it seemed to butt up against the east face of Wall D.4:32 to form a corner. Locus D.4:30a consisted of several poorly preserved plaster layers which seemed to seal up against Walls D.4:31 and D.4:32. Beneath them was the well preserved D.4:33 plaster layer (exposed but not excavated), which did seal up against the walls. Loci D.4:30a and D.4:33 were both cut off to the south by the D.4:2, 13 Ayyūbid/Mamlūk structure.

---

[10] Locus B.4:116 was a similar Late Roman layer which lay between Wall B.4:71 and Wall B.4:155.

*1973 Description (Soil Samples):* Soil samples were taken from the white material in the B.2:24b plaster layer of Stratum 10, and from the white material in the B.2:31c plaster layer of Stratum 11.

*1973 Description (Bones):* The Late Roman Loci produced the following bones in 1973:

| | | | | | |
|---|---|---|---|---|---|
| Sheep/Goat | 96 | Large Mammal | 2 | Snail | 4 |
| Cattle | 9 | Poss. Pig | 1 | | |

*1973 Description (Artifacts):* The latest pottery from the above Loci was Late Roman, and an A.D. 218-222 coin came from Locus B.4:113 (Object 1522).[11] In addition, the Late Roman Loci produced the following registered artifacts:

| | | | | | |
|---|---|---|---|---|---|
| B.4:112 | 1413 | Stone Spindle Whorl | D.4:34 | 1627 | Glass Bead |
| B.4:116 | 1420 | Bronze Bowl Rim | D.4:34 | 1682 | Plaster Fragment |

*1973 Interpretation:* The D.4:34,36 rock tumble would seem to represent the partial collapse of Wall D.4:32 onto the Stratum 10 plaster layer to the west. This collapse could reflect a destruction by earthquake,[12] or it could reflect a major architectural restructuring of the Area prior to the laying of the Early Byzantine Stratum 9 roadway layer (cf. the Stratum 9 robbing of Wall B.4:46).

The Strata 10 and 11 plaster and soil layers could still be interpreted as roadway layers, like Early Byzantine Strata 5-9. The layers would have been bounded by Wall B.4:46 on the south, and by Wall D.4:32 on the east (Stratum 10 only?), while in the west they could have stopped in B.6, or extended further west beyond that point (cf. above, Early Byzantine Strata 5-9). To the north, it would seem that the Stratum 10 plaster layer extended into D.3 to meet the Late Roman stairway, which ascended from D.3 towards the top of the acropolis. In southern B.4, if the B.4:71, 155, 156 walls formed a stairway (cf. below, Early Roman Stratum 12), that stairway could have provided access to the roadway from the south.

If the B.4:71, 155, 156 walls did not form a stairway, they could have belonged to a structure which was located to the south of the main roadway area. In northeastern D.4, the D.4:32 and D.4:31 walls could have formed the corner of another struc-

---

[11] Note also the A.D. 138-161 coin (Object 1521) which came from cleanup Locus B.3:49 (cf. above, n. 3).

[12] Cf. D. H. Kallner-Amiran, "A Revised Earthquake-Catalogue of Palestine," *IEJ* 1 (1950-51): 225 (A.D. 306?).

ture, which lay to the east of the main roadway area. These two Late Roman structures could have belonged either to Stratum 10 or to Stratum 11.

The A.D. 218-222 coin from B.4:113 would agree with the ca. A.D. 135-324 date which was suggested in 1971 for the Late Roman remains of Strata 10 and 11.

### Early Roman Strata 12-13 (ca. 63 B.C. - A.D. 135)

*1968, 1971:* Early Roman remains of Strata 12 and 13, cut into by Ayyūbid/ Mamlūk Stratum 3 and by Early Byzantine Strata 4 and 9, were attested beneath the Late Roman remains of Stratum 11 in 1968 and 1971.

Stratum 12 consisted of the earliest Area-wide plaster layers, which rested on an Early Roman mixed soil and rock tumble layer. Associated with the first (earliest) Stratum 12 plaster layer was a "curbing" (B.4:72 = B.3:31), which ran north-south from B.4 through B.3. Wall B.4:46 was partially robbed out by early Byzantine Stratum 9, but it would originally have retained the Stratum 12 plaster and soil layers on the south. The leveling operation for the Stratum 12 layers would have damaged the remains of earlier Strata 13-16.

Stratum 13 lay beneath the Stratum 12 mixed layer, and it was damaged by the leveling operation for that stratum. It was an Early Roman occupational stratum, the tattered remains of which included soil layers in Cave B.4:74, the B.4:66 *Ṭabun*, and the possible Wall B.4:73.[13] Bedrock cracks through Cave B.4:74 and through bedrock in B.3 suggested that the Early Roman Stratum 13 occupation experienced a major earthquake, and while post-earthquake remains were attested in 1971, pre-earthquake remains were not yet clearly exposed through excavation.

*1973 Description (Stratification):* Additional remains of Early Roman Stratum 12 and Stratum 13 (post-earthquake and pre-earthquake) were attested in Area B (B.2, B.3, B.4, and probably B.6) in 1973.

The Stratum 12 Area-wide plaster layers were attested in Balk-B.2, where the thin B.2:31e-h plaster layers lay beneath the Late Roman layers of Stratum 11. In B.6, the Stratum 12 plaster layers would also probably be included in the B.6:5, 4 layer (cf. above, Early Byzantine Stratum 5). In Balk-B.2, the plaster layers rested on the Stratum 12 mixed layer (B.2:76, 85, 86, 93), and remnants of this mixed layer were also attested in the

---

[13] *Ṭabun* B.2:54 and soil Layer B.2:63, tentatively attributed to Stratum 13 in 1971, should probably be associated with plaster Layer B.2:77 of Stratum 14 (cf. below, n. 19).

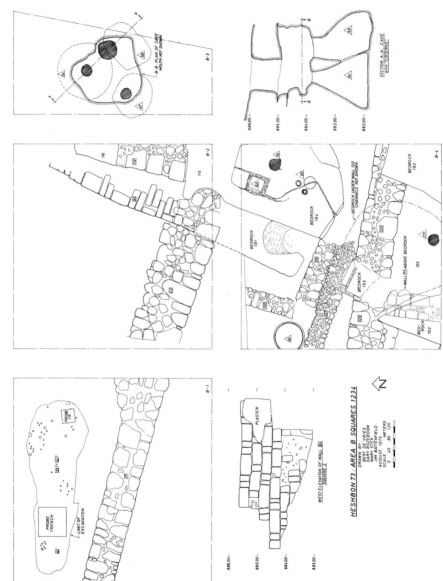

Fig. 4. Composite, selective plan of Squares B.1, B.2, B.3, and B.4. Note also the elevation of Wall B.2:84, and the section of "Cisterns" B.3:59 and 64.

B.3 cave (B.3:55, 56, 57), in southern B.3 (B.3:72, 73, 79), and in northern B.4 (B.4:78, 80). In these sectors, the Stratum 12 mixed layer covered over the Early Roman remains of Stratum 13, the Hellenistic remains of Strata 14, 15, 16, and the Iron I remains of Stratum 19, as well as Bedrock B.2:114a, 116, B.3:84, 85, 86, 87, and B.4:194.

In southern B.4, Wall B.4:46 of Stratum 12 was partially robbed out by Early Byzantine Stratum 9, but its preserved portion still retained the Stratum 12 mixed layer on the north. Wall B.4:46 was built on top of a ca. 1.25 m. thick foundation wall, Wall B.4:120,[14] which also ran east-west through southern B.4. Wall B.4:120, surviving ca. .50-1.25 m. deep, abutted Bedrock B.4:192 and B.4:195, and it ran over Bedrock B.4:195 (including Channels B.4:168) and Plaster B.4:161 (Iron II/Persian Stratum 18) to butt up against and run past Bedrock B.4:193. Between Bedrock B.4:195 and Bedrock B.4:193 the wall rested on top of the Stratum 12 mixed layer (B.4:165; partially excavated).

South of Wall B.4:46/120, the wall was butted up against by three parallel north-south walls (B.4:71, 155, 156). The surviving tops of the three walls were stepped down like a stairway from west to east, and while they were constructed of roughly cut stones as found within the Square, they were constructed of large (ca. .40-.75 m.) finely squared stones as seen in the south balk. There were pockets of soil between the three walls (B.4:151, 153, 157, 158, 159, 160, 164), and the walls were built over Bedrock B.4:192 and Plaster B.4:161 (Iron II/Persian Stratum 18), as well as on the Early Roman Stratum 12 mixed layer (B.4:163, 167, above Bedrock B.4:195 and Channels B.4: 168).

In the southwest corner of B.4, beneath the B.4:129 Late Roman layer, Layers B.4:131, 132 sealed up against Wall B.4:46 and Wall B.4:71. Beneath these layers was the Stratum 12

[14] Wall B.4:120E lay east of Bedrock B.4:192, 195, while Wall B.4:120W lay west of Bedrock B.4:192, 195. Several stones of what later was clearly part of Wall B.4:120W were originally termed Locus B.4:135.

mixed layer (B.4:134, 136, 138), partially excavated, which sealed against Wall B.4:120 and Bedrock B.4:192.

In the southeast corner of B.4, beneath the B.4:112, 113, 119 Late Roman layers, Layer B.4:122 sealed against Wall B.4:120 and Wall B.4:156, and it ran over Bedrock B.4:193. Beneath Layer B.4:122 was the Stratum 12 mixed layer (B.4:117, 123, 125, 133, 137, 139, 162), partially excavated, which covered over Bedrock B.4:195, Channels B.4:168, and Cave B.4:171.

North of Wall B.4:46/120, to the east, the Stratum 12 mixed layer (B.4:94, 106, 107, 111, 146, 166), partially excavated, filled the space between Wall B.4:120 and Bedrock B.4:194. To the west, the Stratum 12 mixed layer (B.4:169, 170), partially excavated, also filled the space between Wall B.4:120 and Wall B.4:73/127.

Stratum 13 Wall B.4:73/127,[15] beneath the Stratum 12 mixed layer, ran into the Square from the west, and it ran eastward somewhat between Bedrock B.4:194 and Bedrock B.4:195. Built against the south face of Wall B.4:115, it was constructed of medium-sized (ca. .25-.40 m.) stones. It was ca. .80 m. thick, survived ca. 1.00 m. high, and rested on a yet unexcavated rock tumble.

To the south, Wall B.4:73/127 was sealed against only by the Stratum 12 mixed layer (B.4:169,170), which filled the space between Wall B.4:120 and Wall B.4:73/127.

To the north, beneath the Stratum 12 mixed layer, Wall B.4:73/127 was sealed against by the Stratum 13 soil Layers B.4: 81, 88, 118, 180, 182, which also sealed against the vertical face of Bedrock B.4:194=B.2:114a, and which continued into B.2 (B.2:96) to seal against the south face of Wall B.2:62. Associated with these Stratum 13 layers in the north balk of B.4 was a square stone installation (B.4:83, 86, 87; B.2:95), which was covered by a plaster layer (B.4:85) that sealed against Bedrock B.4:194=B.2:114a and Wall B.2:62. Ṭabun B.4:66 and Ṭabun B.4:84, next to Wall B.4:73/127, were also associated with the layers. Ṭabun B.4:66 was sealed against by Layer B.4:81, and it

[15] Locus B.4:148 was the soil within Wall B.4:73/127, during the initial dismantling of its upper courses.

lay above Wall B.4:115. *Ṭabun* B.4:84, containing soil and ash Layers B.4:140, 141, 142, 143, 145, was sealed against by Layer B.4:88, and its B.4:121 foundation trench cut down into the Stratum 13 soil layers below (B.4:89, 90, 98, 126, 172). Next to *Ṭabun* B.4:84 was a jar (B.4:174), containing Loci B.4:175, 176, 178, which apparently cut down into Walls B.4:115 and B.4:100.

Stratum 13 Walls B.4:115 and B.4:100 lay beneath and were apparently cut into by the Stratum 13 Loci associated with Wall B.4:73/127. Wall B.4:115 ran east-west flush against the north face of Wall B.4:73/127, from the damaged corner with Wall B.4:100 eastward to the southwest corner of vertically faced Bedrock B.4:194. The wall, constructed of medium-sized (ca. .25-.40 m.) stones, was ca. .75 m. thick and survived ca. 1.00 m. high, and while it was founded in the east on Bedrock B.4:191, in the west it had a foundation trench (B.4:149) which cut down into Layers B.4:150, 173 of Hellenistic Stratum 16. North-south Wall B.4:100 ran northward from the damaged corner with Wall B.4:115 through to Square B.2 (B.2:106), where it butted up against the south face of Wall B.2:62. The wall, constructed of small and medium sized (ca. .15-.40 m.) stones, was ca. .60 m. thick and survived ca. .50 m. high, and it rested on top of Layers B.4:150, 173 of Hellenistic Stratum 16.

Inside the Stratum 13 "room" formed by Wall B.4:115, Wall B.4:100=B.2:106, Wall B.2:62, and vertical bedrock Face B.4:194=B.2:114a, numerous patchy soil layers (B.4:95, 96, 97, 103, 104, 105, 108, 109, 114, 128; B.2:98, 101) lay on top of the well preserved B.4:102=B.2:99 cobblestone pavement. Beneath the cobblestone pavement were several layers of soil and rock tumble (B.4:147, 152, 186), which covered over Bedrock B.4:191= B.2:114b (Iron II/Persian Stratum 18).

To the west of Stratum 13 Wall B.4:100=B.2:106, several soil layers sealed against that wall and against Wall B.2:62 (B.4:89, 90, 98, 126, 172; B.2:102, 103, 104). These layers, cut into by the B.4:121 foundation trench of *Ṭabun* B.4:84, lay above Layers

B.4:150, 173 and B.2:108 (partially excavated) of Hellenistic Stratum 16.

Occupational remains of Early Roman Stratum 13 were also attested in two caves in B.4.

In northeastern B.4, the opening to Cave B.4:74 was found in cracked Bedrock B.4:194, beneath the Stratum 12 mixed layer. Near the opening were two bedrock-cut installations, the B.4:99 cupmarks and the B.4:101 rectangular depression. Beneath Bedrock B.4:194, the B.4:74 cave had a surviving height of ca. 1.50 m., and an overall size of ca. 3.00-4.00 m. Wall B.4:198, constructed of large (ca. .40-.80 m.) stones, formed the boundary of the cave on the east and the south. The cave was filled almost to its opening with a number of superimposed Stratum 13 soil layers (B.4:54=91, 59=92=154, 62=93, 63=110, 64=124, 67=130, 67=144=185=189), which sloped down from the opening to Wall B.4:198 south and east in the cave. The lower layers (B.4:63=110 ff.) were more horizontal within the cave, and Layer B.4:67=130 appeared as white straw-like material. Beneath Layer B.4:67=144 in the northern portion of the cave was the ca. .70 m. round opening to "Cistern" B.4:188, which was cut into the cave floor Bedrock B.4:196. The "cistern" was only partially excavated in 1973 (Layers B.4:184, 187).

In southern B.4, beneath the Stratum 12 mixed layer (B.4:162), the ca. .40 m. diameter opening to Cave B.4:171 was found cut into Bedrock B.4:195. Because the surface of Bedrock B.4:195 sloped down sharply to the east (broken off from bedrock Blocks B.4:192, 193, 194), the cave had a pinched off surviving height of ca. .35-1.00 m., and a reduced floor space of ca. 1.50-3.00 m. The opening to the cave was blocked by a large stone, and inside the cave the three superimposed Stratum 13 soil layers (B.4:177, 179, 181), which covered cave floor Bedrock B.4:197, did not fill the cave up to the level of the opening. There may have been walls on the west and the north sides of the cave, supporting Bedrock B.4:195 from underneath.

*1973 Description (Soil Samples):* Soil samples were taken from the lining in the B.4:84 *tabun*, and from the white straw-like material in the B.4:67 = 130 layer, both of which belonged to Stratum 13.

*1973 Description (Bones):* The Early Roman Loci of Strata 12 and 13 produced the following bones in 1973:

| | | | | | |
|---|---|---|---|---|---|
| Sheep/Goat | 272 | Large Mammal | 9 | Domestic Chicken | 5 |
| Cattle | 39 | Pig | 2 | Wild Bird | 4 |
| Donkey | 4 | Cat | 1 | Rodent | 3 |
| Poss. Camel | 4 | Small Mammal | 2 | Snail | 7 |

These bones were fairly evenly distributed among the Early Roman Loci of Strata 12 and 13. It should be noted, however, that the two pig bones came from Loci B.4:91 and B.4:94, and that the four possible camel bones came from Locus B.4:141 (inside the B.4:84 *tabun*).

*1973 Description (Artifacts):* The latest pottery from the above Loci was Early Roman. While the Stratum 12 plaster layers continued to produce only small quantities of Early Roman pottery, which could not be closely dated, the Stratum 12 mixed layer produced large quantities of Early Roman II-III (ca. 37 B.C. - A.D. 73) pottery. Early Roman II-III pottery also came from the Stratum 13 Loci associated with Wall B.4:73/127 and from the upper Stratum 13 layers (B.4:54 = 91, 59 = 92 = 154, 62 = 93) in Cave B.4:74. Early Roman I (ca. 63-37 B.C.) pottery came from the Stratum 13 Loci associated with Walls B.4:115 and B.4:100, from the lower Stratum 13 layers (B.4:63 = 110 ff.) in Cave B.4:74, and from the Stratum 13 layers in Cave B.4:171.

A 9 B.C. - A.D. 40 coin (Object 1646) came from Locus B.3:72, from the Stratum 12 mixed layer. Another 9 B.C. - A.D. 40 coin (Object 1645) came from Wall B.4:120, the foundation wall beneath Wall B.4:46, which retained the Stratum 12 mixed layer. From Locus B.5:105, a Stratum 13 layer associated with Walls B.4:115 and B.4:100, came an early 1st century B.C. coin (Object 1644). From Locus B.4:124, a Stratum 13 layer inside Cave B.4:74, came a 40-37 B.C. coin (Object 1523).

In addition, the Early Roman Loci of Strata 12 and 13 produced the following registered artifacts:

| | | | | | |
|---|---|---|---|---|---|
| B.3:56 | 1446 | Glass Bead | B.4:120 | 1668 | Greek Ostracon[15a] |
| B.3:73 | 1601 | Basalt Mace | B.4:127 | 1636 | Grinding Stone |
| B.4:94 | 1351 | Iron Nail | B.4:130 | 1433 | Grinding Stone |
| B.4:94 | 1367 | Door Socket | B.4:169 | 1622 | Stone Bead |
| B.4:94 | 1384 | Iron Spike | B.4:175 | 1667 | Millstone |
| B.4:94 | 1389 | Ivory Pin | B.4:186 | 1671 | Clay Loomweight |
| B.4:105 | 1463 | Lamp | B.4:186 | 1683 | Stone Bowl |
| B.4:118 | 1405 | Stone Bowl | | | |

*1973 Interpretation:* Although there was apparently no evidence for a stairway in Area D until the Late Roman period (cf. above, Stratum 10), the Early Roman Stratum 12 plaster layers could still be interpreted (like Late Roman Stratum 11) as

[15a] Bastiaan Van Elderen, "A Greek Ostracon from Heshbon: Heshbon Ostracon IX," *AUSS* 13 (1975): 21-22.

roadway layers in Area B. It would seem that Wall B.4:46/120 was built during the construction of the roadway, south of Wall B.4:73/127 over the Stratum 12 mixed layer and cracked bedrock. The Stratum 12 mixed layer would have filled in the spaces next to Wall B.4:46/120, and leveled up the roadway sector for the laying of the first Stratum 12 plaster layer. Walls B.4:71, 155, 156 could have formed a stairway providing access to the roadway from the south. The two 9 B.C.-A.D. 40 coins from Stratum 12 would agree with the ca. A.D. 70 date which was suggested in 1971 for the original construction date of the roadway. The construction and use of the Stratum 12 plaster layers could thus probably be dated to ca. A.D. 70-135.

Beneath the Stratum 12 roadway would have been the Stratum 13 Early Roman occupation, which was more extensive in Area B than had been anticipated in 1971. However, unless the Stratum 13 remains were scraped off north of Wall B.2:62 during the Stratum 12 roadway leveling operation, this occupation would have been confined to the area south of Wall B.2:62. It would seem that the Stratum 13 occupation built up after cutting along the south face of Wall B.2:62, reusing that Hellenistic Stratum 14 wall, and it may also have cleaned out Hellenistic Stratum 15 remains from Caves B.4:74 and B.4:171 (cf. below). Stratum 13 also cut down into the Hellenistic Stratum 16 layers, exposing the bedrock edge (B.4:191) of Iron II/Persian Stratum 18. Stratum 13 would seem to have been a domestic occupation, to judge from its minor walls, *tabuns*, and other installations. The occupation would have been interrupted by an earthquake, and both the post-earthquake and the pre-earthquake remains were found in Area B in 1973.

The post-earthquake Stratum 13 remains would consist of Wall B.4:73/127, its associated Loci, and the upper soil layers (B.4:54=91, 59=92=154, 62=93) in Cave B.4:74. Since Wall B.4:73/127 was built between Bedrock B.4:194 and Bedrock B.4:195, it would postdate the earthquake which cracked open

those bedrock blocks, and it would seem to have replaced
Wall B.4:115. The upper soil layers in Cave B.4:74 filled up that
cave almost to the level of its opening, and they would seem to
have been dumped into the cave after its B.4:194 bedrock ceiling
was cracked by the earthquake. South of Wall B.4:73/127 there
would not seem to have been any post-earthquake Stratum 13 occupation, unless its remains were removed during the Stratum 12
construction of Wall B.4:46/120.

The pre-earthquake Stratum 13 remains would consist of Walls
B.4:115 and B.4:100=B.2:106, and their associated Loci, the
lower layers (B.4:63=110 ff.) in Cave B.4:74, and the layers in
Cave B.4:171. Wall B.4:100=B.2:106 could be compared with
Wall B.1:25,[16] and these walls could have formed a series of rooms
against the south face of Wall B.1:17=B.2:62. Bedrock would
have been connected, forming the ceilings of (dry storage?)
Caves B.4:74 and B.4:171 until it was cracked by the earthquake
into large blocks (B.4:191/194, 192, 193, 195).[17] Bedrock Block
B.4:195 would have collapsed to the east, breaking off from Bedrock B.4:194 and B.4:193, and it would have pinched off the
opening to Cave B.4:171. Cave B.4:171 would not have been used
again after the earthquake, while Cave B.4:74, only cracked by
the earthquake, would have remained open and been filled up
gradually. The 40-37 B.C. coin from Layer B.4:124, inside Cave
B.4:74, would agree perfectly with the 31 B.C. date which was
suggested in 1971 for the Stratum 13 earthquake. The post-
earthquake Stratum 13 occupation could thus probably be dated
to ca. 31 B.C. - A.D. 70. The pre-earthquake Stratum 13 occupation
could probably be dated to ca. 63-31 B.C., although it could have
begun earlier in the 1st century B.C. (cf. the early 1st century B.C.
coin which came from Layer B.4:105).

[16] Wall B.1:25 was assigned to undated Stratum 14 in 1971.

[17] The bedrock ceiling of the B.3 cave would also have been cracked by the
earthquake into large blocks (B.3:84, 85, 87). Cf. below, Late Hellenistic
Stratum 15.

## Late Hellenistic Strata 14, 15, 16 (ca. 198-63 B.C.)

*1968, 1971:* In addition to the Early Roman occupation of Stratum 13, the undated walls of Stratum 14, the Late Hellenistic remains of Stratum 15, and the Iron II/Persian rock tumble and soil layers of Stratum 16 lay beneath the Early Roman mixed layer of Stratum 12 in 1968 and 1971. Stratum 14 consisted primarily of Wall B.1:17 = B.2:62, which cut down into Stratum 16.[18] Stratum 15 consisted of two soil pockets and an unexcavated "cistern" (B.3:47) in B.3. And Stratum 16 consisted of a ca. 6.50 m. deep (partially excavated) rock tumble and soil layer accumulation in B.1, which also appeared in B.2 and possibly in the northwest corner of B.3.

*1973 Description (Stratification):* Additional remains of Strata 14, 15, and 16 were found in Area B in 1973, and the new evidence would suggest that Strata 14 and 15 were contemporary Late Hellenistic accumulations, and that Stratum 16 was deposited by an earlier Hellenistic operation.

Wall B.1:17=B.2:62 of Stratum 14 ran east-west through B.1 and B.2, beneath the Early Roman mixed layer of Stratum 12. Constructed of large (ca. .25-1.50 m.) stones, it was ca. 1.10 m. thick in B.1 and ca. 1.80 m. thick in B.2. Its foundation trench (B.1:40, 103; B.2:69, 105) was cut down into the Stratum 16 layers, ca. 4.75 m. deep in B.1, and ca. 1.75 m. deep (partially excavated) in B.2. The wall butted up against vertical bedrock Face B.2:114a, and it partially covered over bedrock Surface B.2:114b and the top of Wall B.2:84 of Iron II/Persian Stratum 18. On the south it was sealed against by the Early Roman remains of Stratum 13, while on the north it was sealed against by a tattered Late Hellenistic layer.

Plaster Layer B.2:77, beneath the Stratum 12 mixed layer in the easternmost portion of B.2, sealed against the vertical west face of Bedrock B.2:116 and Wall B.2:112 of Iron I Stratum 19. The layer sloped upward to the south, but it was shaved off by the Stratum 12 leveling operation just before it reached the north face of Wall B.2:62. Beneath Layer B.2:77 was a mixed soil layer (B.2:78, 88, 89, 90, 91, 109) which sealed against Walls B.2:62 and

---

[18] Stratum 14 also included Wall B.1:27 and Walls B.1:21, 25, 28 in 1971. Wall B.1:25 has now been assigned tentatively to Stratum 13, while the other walls remain undated.

B.2:112, and which partially covered over the layers of Stratum 16 and Wall B.2:84 of Stratum 18. Two storage jars were associated with the B.2:77 plaster layer.[19] Jar B.2:82, intact, had a foundation trench (B.2:87) which was cut down into Wall B.2:84. The jar's body was buried in the mixed layer beneath Layer B.2:77, and its neck was sealed against by plaster Layer B.2:77. A small rock covered the mouth of the jar, and the jar contained very little soil. Jar B.2:75, containing Soil B.2:110, rested near Wall B.2:62 in the mixed soil layer beneath Layer B.2:77, but its upper portion was shaved off by the Stratum 12 leveling operation.

In central B.3, bedrock Blocks B.3:84, 85, 87 formed the fractured roof and opening to a cave. The cave had a height of ca. 1.00-1.50 m., and an irregular size of ca. 2.00-3.00 m. Beneath the Stratum 12 mixed layer inside the cave were three Late Hellenistic Stratum 15 "cisterns" (B.3:47, 59, 64). The three "cisterns" were cut into the bedrock floor of the B.3 cave, and on that floor there was a single soil layer (B.3:71) associated with them.

"Cistern" B.3:47 was cone-shaped, with a ca. .40 m. diameter circular opening, a ca. 1.60 m. diameter circular floor, and a ca. 1.75 m. height. Toolmarks were clearly visible on the walls of the "cistern," and the southern wall attested blocking stones (B.3:69) which filled a space where the "cistern" had broken through bedrock Blocks B.3:84, 85 into the Iron I layers of Stratum 19. The opening to the "cistern" was covered with a capstone, and the "cistern" contained only several soil layers (B.3:50, 51, 52) on its bottom.

"Cistern" B.3:59, northeast of "Cistern" B.3:47, was also cone-shaped, but it was cut off-center towards the east. It had a ca. .65 m. diameter circular opening, a ca. 1.65 m. diameter irregular floor, and a ca. 2.10 m. height. The "cistern" walls again attested clear toolmarks, and the western bedrock wall attested

[19] *Tabun* B.2:54 and soil Layer B.2:63, tentatively assigned to Stratum 13 in 1971, could also probably be associated with the B.2:77 plaster layer.

stones (B.3:65) which blocked a space where "Cistern" B.3:59 and "Cistern" B.3:64 intersected. The opening to "Cistern" B.3:59 was not covered with a capstone, and the "cistern" was filled to the top with a number of superimposed soil layers (B.3:58, 60, 61, 62, 63, 66). The lowest layer (B.3:66) consisted of a thin gray straw-like deposit above the bedrock floor of the "cistern."

"Cistern" B.3:64, northwest of "Cistern" B.3:59, was cone-shaped, with a ca. .40 m. diameter circular opening, a ca. 2.00 m. diameter circular floor, and a ca. 2.00 m. height. Toolmarks were clearly visible, and the "cistern" intersected "Cistern" B.3:59 on the east. The opening to the "cistern" was blocked with a cap-stone (B.3:70), and the "cistern" contained only two thin soil layers (B.3:67, 68) on the bottom. Layer B.3:68 was similar to Layer B.3:66 in "Cistern" B.3:59.

Stratum 16 was attested in B.1, B.2, and northwestern B.4, and possibly also in northwestern B.3. It lay beneath and was disturbed by Early Roman Stratum 12 in B.1 and B.2, and it was cut into by Early Roman Stratum 13 in southern B.2 and B.4. It was also cut into and sealed over by Late Hellenistic Stratum 14 in eastern B.2, and possibly also in northwestern B.3

The Stratum comprised sloping soil and rock tumble layers, which were ca. 7.00 m. deep in B.1, and ca. 2.00-3.00 m. deep (partially excavated) in B.2. In B.4, the layers were only touched beneath Early Roman Stratum 13, while in B.3 the stratum included only several possible soil Loci above Bedrock B.3:38.

The uppermost rock tumble and soil layers of Stratum 16, sloping down westward, were attested in B.2 (B.2:72, 73, 74, 79, 80, 81, 83),[20] and possibly also in northwestern B.3 (B.3:54, 53). In northern B.2, the B.2:83 rock tumble layer sealed over and against Wall B.2:84 of Iron II/Persian Stratum 18, and this layer possibly continued into B.3 as Loci B.3:54, 53.

Beneath the uppermost rock tumble and soil layers of Stratum

[20] A single A.D. 2nd-4th century coin (Object 1538) came from early morning cleanup of Locus B.2:80. It should be considered intrusive.

16 was a deep (ca. 1.00-2.00 m.) soil layer, which contained numerous thin layers of soil and black ash (B.1:127, 129, 130, 131, 132, 133, 134, 135, 136, 137, 138=122, 139=123, 140=124, 141=125;[21] B.2:92, 94, 100, 107, 108, 111; B.4:150, 173). The Stratum 16 layer sloped down sharply westward, and it sealed against Wall B.2:84, bedrock vertical Face B.2:114b, and bedrock vertical Face B.4:191 (the eastern wall of the Iron II/Persian Stratum 18 "reservoir").

The thick Stratum 16 soil layer tapered out in the western portion of B.1 between rock Tumble B.1:94 and rock Tumble B.1:118=126=142. Rock Tumble B.1:118=126=142 was ca. 1.00-2.00 m. deep and contained large (ca. .25-.75 m.) squared and unsquared stones which had numerous air pockets between them. Despite its depth, the tumble contained relatively little pottery (ca. 120 registered sherds). The Stratum 16 tumble rested on top of the Iron II/Persian clay Layer B.1:119=143 of Stratum 17, which covered over the Iron II/Persian "cement" Layer B.1:121= 144 of Stratum 18 (the floor of the "reservoir").

*1973 Description (Bones):* The Late Hellenistic Loci of Strata 14 and 15 produced the following bones in 1973:

| Sheep/Goat | 36 | Domestic Chicken | 2 | Snail | 1 |
| Large Mammal | 2 | Wild Bird | 6 | | |

The bones from Stratum 16 have been included with the Iron II/Persian bone evidence (cf. below).

Fig. 5A.   Hellenistic sherd from rock Tumble
B.1:142. Scale 1:2. Color: 7.5R 6/8 (light red).

*1973 Description (Artifacts):* The latest pottery from the Loci of Strata 14 and 15 was Late Hellenistic. The Stratum 16 layers produced essentially pure Iron II/Persian pottery, but a single clear Hellenistic sherd (Figure 5A)

---

[21] These Loci also equal Loci excavated in other parts of B.1 in 1968 and 1971 (cf. Fig. 5). Locus B.1:120 was balk trim.

came from the Stratum 16 rock Tumble B.1:142.[22] No relevant coins or stamped jar handles were attested in 1973, but the following registered artifacts came from the Loci of Strata 14 and 15 in 1973:

| | | | | | | |
|---|---|---|---|---|---|---|
| B.2:75 | 1679 | Glass Bead | B.3:62 | 1399 | Bone Spatula |
| B.2:82 | 1455 | Slingstone | B.3:62 | 1400 | Ornamental Bone |
| B.3:58 | 1358 | Stone Bowl | B.3:62 | 1406 | Door Socket |
| B.3:58 | 1359 | Iron Strip | B.3:62 | 1418 | Bone Spatula |
| B.3:58 | 1364 | Small Bronze Hook | B.3:62 | 1427 | Granite Macehead |
| B.3:61 | 1382 | Iron Nail | B.3:67 | 1444 | Cosmetic Palette |
| B.3:61 | 1474 | Lamp | B.3:70 | 1487 | Slingstone |
| B.3:61 | 1475 | Ceramic Plate | | | |

The artifacts from Stratum 16 have been included with the Iron II/Persian artifacts (cf. below).

*1973 Interpretation:* The Stratum 14 B.1:17=B.2:62 wall could still probably be interpreted as a defensive structure at the base of the acropolis. On the north side of the wall, the B.2:77 plaster layer was associated with Wall B.2:112 of Iron I Stratum 19; that layer would probably reflect reuse of Wall B.2:112 and primary use of Wall B.1:17=B.2:62. On the south side of Wall B.1:17=B.2:62, either there would have been no occupational use of the wall, or the remains there (including remains in Caves B.4:74 and B.4:171?) would have been removed by Early Roman Stratum 13.

The Stratum 15 B.3:47, 59, 64 "cisterns" in the B.3 cave probably would have been contemporary with Stratum 14 B.1:17= B.2:62 wall, although there was no direct stratigraphic connection excavated between them. "Cistern" B.3:64 would have predated slightly "Cistern" B.3:59, since "Cistern" B.3:59 was cut into it and was then dug off-center to the east. Since the walls of the "cisterns" were unplastered, and since toolmarks, bedrock cracks, and blocking stones were also found, the "cisterns" could not have held water, and they would probably have been used to store dry materials (straw? cf. Loci B.3:66, 68) instead.

The Stratum 16 soil and rock tumble layers could now, on the basis of the Hellenistic sherd which came from rock Tumble B.1:142, be interpreted as a massive fill which was dumped into

---

[22] The sherd could not have been intrusive, since it was observed in the field by the Square Supervisors, James Battenfield and Adib Abu-Schmais.

Area B early in the Hellenistic period (prior to Stratum 14). Since only tattered Iron II/Persian remains were recovered above bedrock on the top of the acropolis, it would seem likely that the Hellenistic occupants cleared off the acropolis and dumped the Iron II/Persian remains into (and, in northern B.2, over) the decaying Iron II/Persian "reservoir" of Strata 17 and 18. Most of the Stratum 16 bones and artifacts would thus probably be Iron II/Persian rather than Hellenistic in date, and thus they have been included below with the Iron II/Persian evidence.

### Iron II/Persian Strata 17, 18 (ca. 700-500 B.C.)

*1968, 1971:* The Stratum 16 soil and rock tumble layers were assigned to the Iron II/Persian period in 1968 and 1971, but they now would seem to have been produced in the Hellenistic period (cf. above). No remains earlier than the Stratum 16 layers were exposed through excavation in 1968 or 1971.

*1973 Description (Stratification):* Beneath the Stratum 16 layers in B.1 was the moist clay layer of Stratum 17, which rested on the thick horizontal "cement" layer of Stratum 18. In eastern B.2 and B.4, the Stratum 16 layers were retained by the Stratum 18 wall and vertical bedrock faces.

In B.1, beneath the B.1:118=126=142 rock tumble of Stratum 16 was the moist gray clay Layer B.1:119=143 of Stratum 17. The clay layer was ca. .30-.40 m. deep and it contained large quantities of pottery (ca. 1000 registered sherds) and other artifacts (cf. below) in addition to small and medium sized rocks.

The clay layer of Stratum 17 rested on top of the horizontal "cement" Layer B.1:121=144 of Stratum 18,[23] which was exposed in a ca. 2.00 x 6.00 m. sector of B.1. The top surface of Layer B.1:121=144 showed forty-two ca. .05-.10 m. diameter cupmarks, eight to the west (B.1:128), and thirty-four to the east (B.1:144a). Two probes (1.00 x 1.00 m., and .50 x .50 m.) into the B.1:121=144 "cement" layer revealed three superimposed gray and yellow "cement" layers (B.1:145=149, 146=150, 147=151),

---

[23] The material in Layer B.1:121 = 144 was much harder and smoother than plaster, and it has thus been termed "cement."

each ca. .08-.10 m. deep, which lay above horizontal bedrock Surface B.1:148=152 (cf. Plate IV:B).

In B.2, beneath the eastern end of Wall B.2:62 and plaster Layer B.2:77 of Late Hellenistic Stratum 14, and beneath and sealed against on the west by the rock tumble and soil layers of Hellenistic Stratum 16, was the Stratum 18 north-south Wall B.2:84 and vertical bedrock Face B.2:114b. On the east, Wall B.2:84 was built against Wall B.2:112 of Stratum 19, and against vertical bedrock Face B.2:116. The wall was constructed of ca. .80 x .22 x .35 m. finely squared stones, and it was laid in an alternating double-header, single-stretcher coursing. During this season, eight surviving courses of the wall were exposed, but in the lower courses some of the stones (B.2:115) were missing. The wall line was exposed for ca. 6.00 m., and at the north balk it seemed to be curving slightly westward. To the south, the wall line continued as vertical bedrock Face B.2:114b, and patches of facing plaster (B.2:113) were found on the west face of both Wall B.2:84 and Bedrock B.2:114b (cf. Plate IV:A).

Bedrock Face B.2:114b and Plaster B.2:113 of Stratum 18 continued into northern B.4 as vertical bedrock Face B.4:191 and Plaster B.4:190, beneath Early Roman Stratum 13, and was sealed against on the west by Hellenistic Stratum 16. Between Bedrock B.4:191 and Bedrock B.4:195 there was a break in the bedrock, which was later filled by Early Roman walls of Stratum 13. Bedrock Surface B.4:195, beneath Early Roman Stratum 12, was tilted down eastward (cf. above, Stratum 13), but it still had plaster preserved on its western, formerly vertical face. On its eastward-tilted surface were found three cut channels (B.4:168), each ca. .12 m. wide, which converged to form a single channel on the west. The southernmost channel ran in the direction of bedrock Surface B.4:193, and that block also preserved the remains of a cut channel. Bedrock Face B.4:195 was tilted slightly out of line from vertical bedrock Face B.4:192, but fractured Plaster B.4:161 still joined them. Bedrock Face B.4:192

continued into the southwest corner of B.4, where it cornered to run west (cf. Plate V:A).

*1973 Description (Soil Samples):* A soil sample was taken from the moist gray material in the B.1:119 clay layer of Stratum 17.

*1973 Description (Bones):* The Iron II/Persian clay Layer B.1:119 = 143 of Stratum 17 produced the following bones in 1973:

| | | | | | |
|---|---|---|---|---|---|
| Sheep/Goat | 215 | Camel | 1 | Large Mammal | 5 |
| Cattle | 31 | Gazelle | 2 | Snail | 1 |
| Donkey | 2 | | | | |

In addition, the following bones came from the rock tumble and soil layers of Stratum 16 (cf. above, Hellenistic):

| | | | | | |
|---|---|---|---|---|---|
| Sheep/Goat | 1242 | Prob. Pig | 5 | Domestic Chicken | 8 |
| Cattle | 63 | Dog | 1 | Wild Bird | 6 |
| Poss. Donkey | 3 | Cat | 8 | U.D. Bird | 2 |
| Gazelle | 6 | Rodent | 2 | Snail | 3 |
| Large Mammal | 3 | Turtle | 1 | | |

*1973 Description (Artifacts):* The dominant (ca. 1000 registered sherds) and latest pottery from the B.1:119 = 143 clay layer of Stratum 17 was Iron II/Persian. The B.1:121 = 144 "cement" layer of Stratum 18, including Layers B.1:145 = 149, 146 = 150, 147 = 151, produced only seven small body sherds, which seemed to be Iron II/Persian or Iron Age. The uppermost course of Stratum 18 Wall B.2:84 produced only Iron II/Persian body sherds. An eleven-line ostracon (Object 1657), dated by Cross to ca. 600 B.C.,[24] came from the B.1.143 clay layer of Stratum 17. In addition, the following registered artifacts came from the Stratum 17 B.1:119 = 143 clay layer:

| | | | | | |
|---|---|---|---|---|---|
| B.1:119 | 1329 | Iron Blade Point | B.1:143 | 1561 | Poss. Ostracon |
| B.1:119 | 1392 | Lamp | B.1:143 | 1576 | Horse Head Figurine |
| B.1:143 | 1547 | Iron Arrowhead | B.1:143 | 1631 | Animal Figurine |

The following registered artifacts came from the rock tumble and soil layers of Stratum 16 (cf. above, Hellenistic).

| | | | | | |
|---|---|---|---|---|---|
| B.2:72 | 1313 | Bowl Base | B.2:74 | 1324 | Copper Bar |
| B.2:72 | 1317 | Grinding Stone | B.2:81 | 1396 | Stone Weight |
| B.2:72 | 1318 | Slingstone | B.2:83 | 1401 | Stone Loomweight |
| B.2:72 | 1343 | Bronze Fibula | B.2:83 | 1404 | Slingstone |
| B.2:72 | 1658 | Ostracon[25] | B.2:83 | 1431 | Slingstone |
| B.2:72 | 1659 | Ostracon[26] | B.2:94 | 1625 | Scarab |
| B.2:73 | 1319 | Grinding Stone | B.2:94 | 1656 | Ostracon[27] |
| B.2:73 | 1320 | Slingstone | B.4:150 | 1461 | Faience Bead |

[24] Cf. F. M. Cross, "Ammonite Ostraca from Heshbon: Heshbon Ostraca IV-VIII," *AUSS* 13 (1975): 17.

[25] *Ibid.*, p. 20.

[26] *Ibid.*, pp. 19, 20.

[27] *Ibid.*, pp. 18, 19; dated ca. seventh century B.C.

*1973 Interpretation:* The B.1:119=143 clay layer of Stratum 17, having yielded many artifacts, could probably be interpreted as a use deposit at the bottom of the Stratum 18 "reservoir" (cf. below). In the Hellenistic period the Stratum 16 soil and rock tumble layers would have been dumped into the "reservoir" on top of the Stratum 17 clay layer.

The B.1:121=144 "cement" layer and the B.2:84 plastered wall and B.2-B.4 bedrock faces could probably be interpreted as parts of a large Stratum 18 water reservoir.

The B.1:121=144 "cement" layer was so thick (ca. .26 m.) that it must have been part of a major installation, and it must have been intended to hold water. Containing Layers B.1:145= 149, 146=150, 147=151, it could have been surfaced three separate times, or it could have been surfaced once with three distinct layers of "cement." Since the layer was horizontal, and since in B.1 it lay ca. 6.50-7.00 m. below the level of the uppermost portion of Wall B.2:84 and the B.2-B.4 bedrock faces, it could be interpreted as the floor of the (ca. 7.00 m. deep) Stratum 18 "reservoir."

Before they would have been cracked by the Stratum 13 earthquake, Wall B.2:84 and vertical bedrock Faces B.2:114b, B.4:191, B.4:195, and B.4:192 would probably have formed the ca. 16 m. long, plastered eastern boundary of the Stratum 18 "reservoir." Before bedrock Block B.4:195 was tilted eastward by the earthquake, Channels B.4:168 would probably have conducted water westward into the "reservoir." Since both Wall B.2:84 and bedrock Block B.4:192 seemed to show possible corner lines to the west, and since the western wall of the "reservoir" was not attested in B.1 (ca. 13 m. from Wall B.2:84), it could be suggested that the "reservoir" was approximately square (16 x 16 m.). Agreeing with this suggestion would be the fact that the Stratum 16 Hellenistic soil and rock tumble layers sloped down westward in B.2, and down eastward in B.1, apparently from the east and west sides of the "reservoir."

The pottery from the B.1:119=143 clay layer of Stratum 17 would suggest that the "reservoir" was used during the Iron II/ Persian (ca. 700-500 B.C.) period. However, the Stratum 18 "reservoir" could have been constructed earlier in the Iron Age, since the pottery from "cement" Layer B.1:121 = 144 and from Wall B.2:84 consisted mostly of Iron Age body sherds. The header-stretcher construction of Wall B.2:84 could be compared with the similar, but finer, 9th-8th century B.C. header-stretcher construction of walls at Samaria.[28] It has been suggested by some that the Stratum 18 "reservoir" could have been one of the pools of Heshbon which was referred to in Canticles 7:5 (traditionally attributed to Solomon).

### Iron I Stratum 19 (ca. 1200-1100 B.C.)

*1968, 1971:* No Iron I remains were attested in Area B in 1968 or 1971.

*1973 Description (Stratification):* In 1973, Iron I remains of Stratum 19 were attested in southern B.3 and possibly in south-eastern B.2.

In southern B.3, beneath the Early Roman mixed layer of Stratum 12, Iron I remains were attested in a ca. 1.50-2.00 m. wide space between vertical bedrock Face B.3:84, 85 on the north, and vertical bedrock Face B.3:86 on the south. The remains consisted of several superimposed soil layers ( B.3:74, 75, 76, 77, 81, 82) which sealed against a possible wall in the west balk (B.3:80), as well as a possible wall in the east balk (B.3:78). Both the layers and the walls sealed against vertical bedrock Face B.3:84, 85 on the north, and against vertical bedrock Face B.3:86 on the south. Wall B.3:80 was constructed of large (ca. .25-.75 m.) stones, while Wall B.3:78 was constructed of small (ca. .10-.20 m.) rocks. The walls and the layers were exposed to a depth of ca. 2.50 m., above unexcavated rock Tumble B.3:83. The Late Hellenistic B.3:47 "cistern" of Stratum 15 broke through Bedrock

---

[28] Cf. J. W. Crowfoot, K. M. Kenyon, E. L. Sukenik, *Samaria-Sebaste I* (London, 1942), pp. 3-8ff., 94ff.; Pls. XII/2, XIII/1, 2, XX/2, XXX/1.

B.3:84, 85 on the south "cistern" perimeter, and it cut into the Iron I remains beneath rock Tumble B.3:83.

In southeastern B.2, beneath the Early Roman mixed layer of Stratum 12, Wall B.2:112 filled the ca. 2.50 m. wide space between vertical bedrock Face B.2:116 on the north, and vertical bed-rock Face B.2:114a on the south. The wall's west face was sealed against by the Late Hellenistic B.2:77 plaster layer of Stratum 14, and beneath that layer it was built against by the Iron II/Persian B.2:84 wall of Stratum 18. Wall B.2:112 was con-structed of large (ca. .60-.75 m.) stones, and while two courses of its surviving west face were exposed through excavation, the wall itself was not dismantled. Since bedrock Block B.2:116 would probably equal bedrock Block B.3:84, 85, and since bed-rock Block B.2:114a would probably equal bedrock Block B.3:86, the construction of Wall B.2:112 could probably be dated, with possible Wall B.3:80, to the Iron I period.

*1973 Description (Bones):* The Iron I Stratum 19 Loci in B.3 produced the following bones in 1973:

| | | | | | |
|---|---|---|---|---|---|
| Sheep/Goat | 51 | Donkey | 2 | Pig | 2 |
| Cattle | 3 | Large Mammal | 9 | Domestic Chicken | 2 |
| Horse | 5 | | | | |

*1973 Description (Artifacts):* The pottery from the above Stratum 19 Loci in B.3 was Iron I, with nothing earlier. The Iron I Loci of Stratum 19 pro-duced no registered artifacts.

*1973 Interpretation:* The Iron I remains of Stratum 19, parti-ally excavated in Area B, were too meager to interpret extensively. The ca. 1.50-2.50 m. wide space between Bedrock B.2:116 = B.3: 84, 85 and Bedrock B.2:114a=B.3:86 could have been a natural bedrock cleft, or it could have been a bedrock channel or pit, intentionally cut in the Iron I period. Wall B.2:112 = B.3:80 could possibly be interpreted as a fortification wall, with the B.3 soil layers as fill behind it, but unless the wall was part of a tower, its north-south orientation would argue against that interpretation.

However, the new evidence for an Iron I occupation in Area

B would agree with the new evidence from Area C, where Iron I layers were also found above bedrock in 1973. The Iron I remains on the top of the acropolis, if any (Areas A, D), could have been scraped off during the Iron II/Persian period, since otherwise more Iron I pottery would normally have been found in the Stratum 16 soil and rock tumble layers.

The Iron I evidence from Areas B and C would seem to reflect a small village occupation at the site, not a large city. This evidence could perhaps be associated with an Israelite settlement,[29] but at the present time it could also be associated with a pre-Israelite[30] or with an early Ammonite settlement.[31] In this context the pig bones from the Iron I Loci of Stratum 19 in Area B should be noted.

[29] For the Israelite settlement of Heshbon, cf. Numbers 32:3, 37; Joshua 13:15-17. To associate the Iron I evidence from Ḥesbân with an Israelite settlement would be to agree with the reconstruction of Albright (cf. *Tell Beit Mirsim*, 1: 53-61), which has been followed by many (cf. G. E. Wright,. "The Archaeology of Palestine," *BANE*, pp. 115-116). However, that reconstruction would not explain the absence at Ḥesbân of Late Bronze evidence, if the Numbers 21:21-31 account of the conquest of Heshbon is taken seriously.

[30] For such a treatment of similar Iron I evidence, cf, J. A. Callaway, "New Evidence on the Conquest of 'Ai," *JBL* 87 (1968): 312-320. This treatment attempts to distinguish between a pre-Israelite Iron I pottery and an Israelite Iron I pottery, but the typological distinctions which are made are not yet convincing. Thus far, there would seem to be only one stratigraphic and typological phase of Iron I at Ḥesbân, which could perhaps be interpreted as pre-Israelite. However, such an interpretation would push the date of the conquest down into the 12th century B.C., and it would not satisfy the need from literary evidence for a post-conquest Israelite settlement at the site.

[31] Similar Iron I pottery has come from several recently excavated sites near Amman. Cf. M. Ibrahim, "Archaeological Excavations at Sahab, 1972," *ADAJ* 17 (1972): 30-31; H. Thompson, "The 1972 Excavation of Khirbet al-Hajjar," *ADAJ* 17 (1972): 59-62. It has also been found in quantity on the surface of Tell Safut, northwest of Amman. For the early history of the Ammonites, cf. Judges 11:4-33, I Samuel 11:1-11. Cf. also G. M. Landes, "The Material Civilization of the Ammonites," *The Biblical Archaeologist Reader, 2*, pp. 70-72; J. Bright, *A History of Israel*, pp. 110, 159, 167.

# AREA C

HENRY O. THOMPSON

American Center of Oriental Research

Amman, Jordan

Of the 1971 work previously reported,[1] Squares 4, 5, and 6 were not excavated in 1973, but work in Squares 1, 2, and 3 was continued. So for the most part the excavations in Area C continued in portions begun in 1968.[2]

## Ayyūbid/Mamlūk Period

Square 1 had been dug to sub-Late Roman levels in 1971. Except for some later material from a small balk cutting, no remains for later periods were reported from this Square in the 1973 season.

In Square 2 most of the remains encountered were earlier than Ayyūbid/Mamlūk occupation. A few sherds of this period left from 1968 were found in Loci C.2:7 and 9, undifferentiated fill layers. A surprise in this square was that Wall C.2:10, dated in 1968 as Late Arabic, produced only Umayyad sherds but none from the later periods.

In Square 3 the Ayyūbid/Mamlūk Soil Layers C.3:14 and 7 were difficult to separate distinctly from the overlying Layer C.3:5, the bottom remnant of a dark soil layer mostly removed in 1968. Locus C.3:11, a rocky black and brown soil layer, lying between Wall C.3:10 and the east balk, had Ayyūbid/Mamlūk sherds as the latest pottery. Locus C.3:15 was a pit or trench extending from the south balk 4.30 m. northward into the Square. Three pails of pottery from the abandonment fill included phases

[1] See H. O. Thompson, "Heshbon 1971: Area C," *AUSS* 11 (1973): 72-88.
[2] See Thompson, "Heshbon 1968: Area C," *AUSS* 7 (1969): 127-142.

of Ayyūbid/Mamlūk materials, and several iron nails, a bead, and a rubbing stone.

Wall C.3:18, surviving in 4 stones, 1 row wide and 1 course high, had appeared in 1968 to be a bottom-course extension of house Wall C.3:3. But it proved to be probably a wide lean-to or a courtyard wall of Ayyūbid/Mamlūk date attached to the house. Locus C.3:17, a dark, pebbly soil extending along the east balk from 1.25 to 4.30 m. from the south balk, about .50 m. maximum width, had pottery dating it to the same period, with some ʿAbbāsid and Umayyad material. An iron arrowhead and miscellaneous glass fragments were found here. This locus may have been part of a pit, or debris caught against the uphill side of the abandoned Umayyad Wall C.3:24. Wall C.3:18 relates chronologically to Wall C.3:3, which in 1971 was noted as the latest phase of Ayyūbid/Mamlūk in Area C. Loci C.3:15 and 17 related to the earlier phases, probably Phase 2 of the North Building reported in 1971. The faunal remains from the five C.3 loci described above included a conch-type seashell and a catfish bone which, like the 1971 Aqaba fishbones, were considered evidence of trade. Presumably local were the sheep/goat, cattle, horse, donkey, and domestic chicken bones.

## ʿAbbāsid Period

In Square 2 ʿAbbāsid material found in Loci 9, 16, 17, 18, 19, and 20 (all apparently fill layers, inter-season cleanup, or balk scrapings) supports the supposition that ʿAbbāsid glazed ware now stratigraphically identifiable was possibly present in 1968 loci but then yet undifferentiated from the Ayyūbid/Mamlūk glazes. These fill layers were presumably not *in situ* but brought in from elsewhere on the mound, yet they represent an ʿAbbāsid presence at *Tell Ḥesbân* not clearly distinguished before this year. Objects from these layers included a bone ornamental skewer, a polished ornamental bone, a slingstone, an inscribed roof tile, a fragment of a saddle quern, and a granite bowl rim. Faunal remains from these layers included sheep/goat, cattle, camel, chicken, donkey, horse, cat, wild bird, turtle, snail, a human tooth, and several unidentified bone fragments.

In Square 3 the 'Abbāsid presence is not so evident. A few sherds were present in Loci C.3:5, 8, and 17 (Ayyūbid/Mamlūk in date) noted above; in Locus C.3:14, a red soil layer in the south and west parts of the Square (dominantly Umayyad); and probably as intrusive in Loci C.3:16 (Byzantine) and C.3:21 (Umayyad). Objects from these loci included glass beads and nails.

## Umayyad Period

A study of the 1971 pottery[3] made possible a new demarcation between Byzantine and Umayyad pottery at Hesbân, making isolation of the latter forms a stronger possibility. In Square 1 this reassessment identified some Umayyad pottery in Loci C.1:32 and 35 in the southwest corner of the Square near Byzantine Wall C.1:8. This suggests that Wall C.1:8 was a terrace wall over which soil bearing Umayyad sherds spilled and slid down the slope westward over the top of Early Roman Wall C.1:40.

In Square 2, Umayyad sherds were present and sometimes dominant in Wall C.2:10 and Soil Layers C.2:18, 19, and 20, described above; also a few in Soil Layer C.2:21 lensing out from the south balk, and with the partial (40%) skeleton of a woman (Locus C.2:23) apparently dumped, disarticulated, along with the fill of Locus C.2:22, underlying Locus C.2:18. In Locus C.2:22 Umayyad pottery was the latest in 10 out of 25 pails. Sheep/goat, cattle, donkey, horse, chicken, and human remains were found in this Square.

In Square 3 a probe trench (Locus C.3:13) allowed identification of five soil layers (Loci C.3:7, 14, 15, 22, and 23). The first two yielded primarily Umayyad ware, as in Locus C.3:21 mentioned above (though the latter had a few 'Abbāsid sherds, probably in-

[3] James A. Sauer, *Heshbon Pottery 1971* (AUM 7, 1973), pp. 39-49.

trusive). Layer C.3:22, under C.3:14, was Umayyad, while Locus C.3:23 below it was Byzantine. Wall C.3:24, a rough construction in the east balk, one row thick and six courses high, of field stones .10-.20 m. in diameter, was dated Umayyad by the pottery found in dismantling the wall. Layer C.3:7 yielded a fragment of a bronze figurine head. Another Umayyad deposit was Locus C.3:25, a .15 m. layer of hard packed soil covering about 2.00 sq. m. in the northeast corner of the excavated portion.

All these soil layers appeared to be natural or manmade fill or dump rather than occupation layers. Fauna included sheep/goat, cattle, chicken, donkey, bird, snail, reptile, catfish, conch shell, and several unidentifiable bone fragments.

Square 4 had yielded extensive Umayyad remains in 1971, concentrated around the cistern; it now appeared that Umayyad occupation did not extend westward down the slope except for the irregular wall in Square C.4:5, also noted in 1971.

### Byzantine Period

In Square 1 a small stub of Wall C.1:8 (apparently a retaining wall on the western slope of the *tell*) was removed from the south balk. The pottery under it confirmed its Byzantine date.

In Square 2, Soil Layer C.2:24, lying throughout the excavated portion down to and around Walls C.2:26, 36, and 38, was a Byzantine accumulation covering abandoned buildings. It contained several fragments of stone bowls and grinders.

In Square 3 Firepit C.3:16 was probably Byzantine with ʿAbbāsid intrusions, as mentioned above. Locus C.3:19, a scattered ash layer along the west balk, probably represented another Byzantine firepit. Locus C.3:20, a soil layer near the west balk, had Byzantine sherds but also Hellenistic and Iron Age deposits. Locus C.3:23 was a soil layer up to .15 m. thick over a considerable part of the excavated sector, similar to the 1971 Byzantine Loci C.4:41-53-54.

A small iron bird was found in Locus C.3:23. Byzantine intrusions were found in other loci. The faunal remains in Squares C.2 and C.3 were sheep/goat, cattle, and chicken.

With the exception of retaining Wall C.1:8 on the brink of the west slope of the *tell,* Byzantine evidence was primarily in layers accumulated during the abandonment of this portion of the *tell,* with occasional camp fires during the period.

### Late Roman Period

In Square C.1 the Late Roman evidence noted in 1971 comprised Wall C.1:12 (southeast corner) and Soil Layer C.1:20 (northwest corner).

In 1973 in Square C.2 the rocky Locus C.2:29 in the west balk, also Late Roman, was probably an extension of Wall C.1:12 (broken), appearing through the intervening balk. C.2:30, a soil layer .50 m. deep along the south balk, extended into the Square behind and level with, but not touching, the surviving top of Wall C.2:36, which was a major segment of a circle extending into the Square about 1.30 m. from the south balk. Layer C.2:30 and the underlying Layers C.2:42 and 43 were Late Roman fill thrown into the pit that had been lined by Wall C.2:36, which may also have been Late Roman but more likely, from ceramic evidence, Early Roman.

In Square C.3 only Locus C.3:31, a soil layer of unclear function in the southeast corner, can be reasonably dated to the Late Roman period.

Faunal remains from this period included sheep/goat and chicken.

In summary: The Late Roman occupation in Area C continued, as in 1968 and 1971, to be sparsely represented.

### Early Roman Period

In 1971 Early Roman remains in Area C were found only in Square C.1—two architectural phases and an intervening soil fill. In 1973 no layers datable to that period were found east (uphill) of Square C.2, though some Early Roman sherds were mixed with later materials in C.3.

In Square C.1, in 1973, Early Roman Walls C.1:40, 63, and 30 were noted as comprising the earlier phase. Wall C.1:30, of unhewn field stones (.15-.50 m. diameter), surviving to a height of 1.50 m., made a butt joint with Wall C.1:63 but formed no part of it. Wall C.1:63 was found to be, with Wall C.1:40, part of a continuous structure, with a break (noted in 1971) where the upper part of Wall C.1:40 was falling downhill to the west. Wall C.1:40/63, of unhewn field stone (.25-.75 m. diameter) laid in rough courses solidly chinked, formed a corner with Wall C.1:49 running to the west. It was founded on bedrock or hard red virgin soil immediately over bedrock. These walls possibly represented the northeast corner of an Early Roman tower, possibly part of city fortifications on the western perimeter of the *tell*. (Pl. VI:A.)

This date for Wall C.1:40/63 was confirmed by Foundation Trench C.1:51, noted in 1971 as an Early Roman layer under Byzantine Wall C.1:8. The east edge of this deep (c. 3.60 m.) but narrow foundation trench followed bedrock contours from the south balk 1.50 m. north and thereafter cut through Iron Age layers. The trench fill yielded nothing later than Early Roman materials.

A small quantity of 1971 Layer C.1:18 remaining under the stub of Byzantine Wall C.1:8 was confirmed as Early Roman but later than Trench C.1:51, and similarly the small portion of Layer C.1:45 (1971) *in situ* under it. The latter had been almost a meter thick in the southeast corner of the square, but lensed out to a few centimeters where it seemed to cover Foundation Trench C.1:51, as shown in the south balk. Irregular soil (Loci C.1:84, 86, 88, and 93) overlay tumbled rock (c. .10-.25 m. diameter) lying 1.00-1.50 m. east of the western edge of bedrock. This suggested that Early Roman deposits lay in that area before the construction of Wall C.1:40/63 with its Foundation Trench C.1:51; this was confirmed by evidence from Layers C.1:10 and 77, also cut by Trench C.1:51. There was insufficient evidence to diagnose the functions of these layers.

In Square C.2 the Early Roman period was indicated by pottery in Soil Layer C.2:27 between Wall C.2:26 (Iron Age) and the north balk; also in the two fill layers (Locus C.2:32 and Locus C.2:37 below it) of a pit or trench in the southwest corner of the Square, extending about 3.00 m. east of the west balk and apparently continuous with earth Layer C.1:45—similar in color, consistency, levels and alignment through the balk. The north edge of this Pit C.2:32/37 seemed to be in line with a vertical line in the east balk of C.1 that appeared between 1971 and 1973, presumably due to weathering. This suggested the presence of a pit or trench, or possibly an earthquake fault. The vertical line was traceable down along the north side of Wall C.2:90 (see below), between it and an earlier adjacent soil layer. The lower portion suggested a cut trench rather than an earthquake fault, but the evidence is ambiguous.

The Early Roman "Wall" C.2:36, noted above, seemed to form the lining, one stone thick, of a pit within the Pit C.2:32/37. As first excavated, the north edge of Pit C.2:32/37, running eastward 1.50 m. from the west balk, appeared to form a foundation trench, which was designated Locus C.2:35. The space between Wall C.2:36 and this north edge was filled with rocks (.10-.35 m. diameter) and soil. Pottery indicated that it was abandoned in Early Roman times. A clay game board (Object No. 1632) was found here. The unhewn boulders of "Wall" (Pit lining) C.2:36 ranged from .50-.85 m. in diameter. Two of them, apparently belonging to the top course, remained visible in the south balk. Smaller rocks (.15-.25 m. diameter) seemed to form a base or foundation (six courses high) under the westernmost rock of Locus C.2:36, and one only three courses high under the easternmost rock. A layer of earth, filled with sherds and stones, lay immediately under the boulders of Locus C.2:36. These configurations suggested a stone-lined pit with "Wall" C.2:36 forming the upper part of the lining. Three irregularly placed stones, probably remains of the topmost preserved course of Wall C.2:36, were on the same level as the two boulders in the south balk but did not join them, and all lay on several centimeters of soil. The next course below, also of three stones, was more regular, as were the next two lower courses. The "fifth course" (?) down, of two rocks, was separated from the fourth by an earth layer .10 m. thick, which suggested that a connection was more likely with Wall C.2:52, laid on earth over bedrock (see below).

Wall C.2:38 seemed to be the eastern end of Walls C.1:14 and 37 (1971 Report). Only two stones (of each of the two surviving courses of Wall C.1:14) extended east of the west balk. Pottery in Locus C.2:33 (the foundation trench on the south face of Wall C.2:38) indicated an Early Roman construction date for the wall, which cut down into earlier layers on the south and east. Its function remained unclear at the end of the season.

Faunal remains from this period included sheep/goat, cattle, horse, donkey, pig, rodent, snail, and some indistinguishable material.

### Hellenistic Period

Although a few Hellenistic sherds were found in 1971, this was a new, extended range of evidence in Area C in 1973 in a number of loci. In C.1, Soil Layers C.1:85 and 87, in the southeast corner of the Square along the east balk, lensed out and were overlain by Loci C.1:84, 86, 88, 92, and 93, which were almost level layers, one above the other, in the southeast corner, the last over bedrock. Layer C.1:89 ran over the lowest course of Wall C.1:90. Each layer was cleared separately, but all were pottery-dated to the Hellenistic period and may have comprised an open hearth. Objects from these loci included a bronze earring, four bone knives or spatulas, a bronze pin, and a loom weight.

In Square C.2 was a rock tumble (Locus C.2:28), with gray soil around the stones, lying against the surviving north face of Wall C.2:26. Its latest pottery suggested a period of Hellenistic accumulation around an earlier abandoned construction. Pit C.2:39, under the west end of Locus C.2:28, was filled with Hellenistic deposit after abandonment. In the north balk it appeared contemporary with Locus C.2:28. Locus C.2:46 was a firepit under the east end of Locus C.2:28, with several thin alternating layers of ash, soil, and organic matter. Objects from these loci included a grinder fragment, a slingstone, a bone bead, and a stone scoop or shovel.

Faunal remains included sheep/goat, cattle, donkey, chicken, snail, and indistinguishable fragments. All evidences suggested sparse temporary habitation on this portion of the *tell* in this period.

### *Late Iron II Period*

The Late Iron II Period (7th-6th centuries B.C.) was detected in Soil Layer C.1:60 in 1971. However, the 1973 excavation of the rest of that locus yielded Iron I pottery at the latest. C.1:101, an Early Roman earth layer (probably equivalent to the 1971 Locus C.1:62), overlay a series of soil layers sloping steeply down westward. The highest of these, Locus C.1:77, was probably also Early Roman, but Loci C.1:78, 79 and 80 were Late Iron II deposits. Loci C.1:77-80 were traced northward from a subsidiary balk cut on a line set down 3.30 m. from and parallel to the south balk. Wall C.1:90, of unhewn stones (.25-.50 m. diameter), extended westward from the east balk, with three courses preserved at the balk. Pottery from the wall interior indicated Late Iron II construction.

In Square C.2, a wall (C.2:26) of undressed stones (.25-.50 m. diameter) survived two courses high and two rows wide with a clearly defined north face, but an irregular south face, suggesting that it had been built against the soil of Locus C.2:25 to the south. It may have been part of Wall C.3:26 (see below). Under Wall C.2:26 ran Locus C.2:31, a packed soil layer apparently identical to Locus C.2:34, which was traced eastward from the west balk. Locus C.2:40, of similar consistency, lay under C.2:34 and throughout most of the excavated sector. Layers C.2:41 and 44 were traceable only in the southeast corner of the Square. The latter was behind a small, irregular Terrace Wall C.2:49 (of stones .10-.25 m. in diameter). Pit C.2:45 cut through Locus C.2:40 as well as a *huwwar* surface (Locus C.2:47) under Locus C.2:40. The latter extended to and partly under Wall C.2:49, which was subsequently dismantled and dated to a Late Iron II construction. Excavation stopped here for the season for most of the Square.

Locus C.2:48, similar to Loci C.2:34 and 40, was partially excavated under Pit C.2:45; it appeared to continue under Surface C.2:47, presumably dating the soil fills immediately under C.2:47 as Late Iron II also. Loci C.2:31/34, 40, and 44 may have been identical to Loci C.3:37, 38, 40, and 41. Their fine grain suggested water-laid silt. Locus C.2:50, under Pit C.2:32/35/37, and Locus C.2:51, under Pit C.2:46, both lying on bedrock, were dated by pottery to Late Iron II. Bedrock was exposed also along the east balk under Locus C.2:44. Wall C.2:52, of undressed stones (.25-.50 m. diameter), probably identical to Wall C.1:90 though somewhat different in appearance, was dismantled at its surviving western end. Latest pottery inside the wall and in the soil under it, down to bedrock, was Late Iron II. Objects from these loci included a broken stone seal depicting a lion, a figurine fragment, a polished bone knife, two slingstones, and a basalt grinder.

In Square C.3, Loci C.3:37, 38, 40 and 41, similar to Loci C.2:31/34, 40, and 44, lay under Loci C.3:39, 36, 35, and 30. The lower layers appeared to be water laid, but the upper suggested rock tumble with soil washed or thrown around them. These layers ran up to Walls C.3:32 and 34 without being cut by foundation trenches; their position and their pottery suggested Late Iron II or earlier construction of these walls. One slingstone came from this location.

Wall C.3:32 seemed to represent two construction phases: The east end (surviving two courses high) was built over rubble which lay on a shelf of bedrock. At the west end (where it survived to a height of 3.50 m. in 11 courses) it was battered (stepped?) and its base followed the contour of bedrock down to a lower shelf. It was built of undressed field stones (.40-.70 m. diameter). The north face was quite distinct, but the south face was irregular, suggesting a battered support laid up against Wall C.3:26. Dismantling the top two courses of Wall C.3:32 left the deep-founded north face and the stepped-down or battered west end, enclosing a rubble core. The latest pottery from inside this construction was Late Iron II, with no ceramic distinctions detectable between the contents of the two ends.[4]

Wall C.3:26 also consisted of two phases: the east end well constructed, but the west end built over rubble. The stones (.25-.85 m. diameter) were larger in the east end, where they were either partly dressed or carefully selected for their roughly rectangular shape. A portion of the west end was dismantled; its latest pottery was Late Iron II, with no discernible distinction from the materials of Wall C.3:32. A few Hellenistic sherds in two pails, possibly coming from the south balk, suggested a Hellenistic accumulation south of Wall C.3:26. This wall may have extended through the west balk and continued in Square 2 as Wall C.2:26. In C.3, Walls C.3:32 and 26 both formed a butt joint with north-south Wall C.3:34, which was built on a slighty higher bedrock shelf than that under the rubble of Wall C.3:32. In turn, the space between C.3:34 and a yet higher shelf eastward was leveled up with stone to form a platform (Surface

___

[4] Editor's note: The director ventured the hypothesis that Wall C.3:34/28 was part of the Iron Age II city wall, and Structure C.3:32/26 was one of the city wall's bastions or towers. Only future excavations of the adjacent areas will show whether this interpretation is correct.

C.3:28) with the still higher shelf in the southeast corner of the Square. Wall C.3:34, built of unhewn boulders (.50-.90 m. diameter) survived 1.00 m. high (two courses at the north end, one at the south). A probe through Wall C.3:34 produced four Iron Age sherds.

A summary of the phasing of the Late Iron Age II walls in Area C is made uncertain by the intervening balks and interrupted stratigraphic sequence. If C.2:26 was a westward extension of C.3:26, this wall was later than C.2:52. Though it is not impossible that the eastern end of C.3:26 was set in from above or from the south (cf. the Hellenistic presence noted above as intrusive), it seems more likely (because of C.2:28, Hellenistic soil *up to* the north face of C.2:26, which was set into or against Late Iron II C.3:25) that C.3:26 was earlier than C.3:32, which seemed to lie battered against it. The latter sequence was certain for the eastern ends of Walls C.3:32 and 26, since both butted against C.3:34, which would therefore seem to be still earlier, or contemporary with either. Stratigraphic factors raise other questions, however. Layers C.2:41, 44, 51, 31/34, 40, and 50, under Wall C.2:26, were similar in color and consistency with C.3 soil layers running up to C.3:32. This suggested that C.2:26 and C.3:26 were later than C.3:32, or that evidences of foundation trenches were missed in excavation.

Wall C.2:52 was constructed earlier than C.2:26, but whether it was built earlier than C.3:34, or even C.3:32, was uncertain. The relationship of C.2:52 and C.1:90 was also of interest. Apparently the Hellenistic occupation fill against Wall C.1:90 and running into the east balk of C.1 ended completely within the 1.00 m. thickness of the balk, for there was no evidence of it in the southwest corner of C.2. The pottery evidence suggested that Wall C.1:90 was built early in the Late Iron II period. The presence of abutting Hellenistic layers allowed a later date for the construction of Wall C.1:90, though our opinion was that the sector was cleaned by the later Hellenistic occupants.

In summary, it is suggested that C.1:90 and C.2:52 were parts of the same wall and are the earliest Iron Age walls in Area C, while the intervening soil fills are later, and that the Walls C.2:26 and C.3:32, 26, and 34 are the latest. The ambiguity of the evidence cited above prevents certainty at this stage of excavation.

Faunal remains included sheep/goat, cattle, donkey, chicken, and snail.

### Iron I Period

In the 1968 and 1971 seasons the known Iron I ceramic corpus was represented by a few sherds mixed in later loci. In 1973 this continued to be the case for Squares C.2 and C.3.

In Square C.1 the jump from Late Iron II to Iron I became evident in Locus C.1:80. The layers leveled a bit to a downward slope toward the west of about .25 degrees. Locus C.1:82 was not initially distinguished in the excavated portions between the east balk and Locus C.1:51 (the foundation trench on the east side of Wall C.1:40/63). In the portion of Locus C.1:82 that was beneath Locus C.1:80 the pottery reading was Iron I. Loci C.1:95, 97, 98, and 99 were soil layers over virgin soil (Locus C.1:100) and bedrock.

These layers (Loci C.1:82, 95, 97-99) formed a soil layer sequence on the south, perhaps having been cut to form a bank against which Wall C.1:90 was built. Though this soil-layer sequence seemed to follow through the east balk into Square C.2, no certain Iron I loci were detected in C.2. The slope of these loci suggested fill layers, natural or man-made, forming a westerly slope on the mound, rather than occupation debris. However, their presence may have related to the possible occupation evidence found in Area B.

# AREA D

LAWRENCE T. GERATY
Andrews University

Excavations of Area D, on the south slope of the acropolis of *Tell Ḥesbân,* were begun (in 1968) as three Squares (a fourth was laid out but not dug) to investigate the apparent southern access to the acropolis from the lower city.[1] In 1971, Squares D.5 and D.6 were added north of Square D.1, to link the structures on the edge of the acropolis with those in Squares A.3/4 at the center of the acropolis. But in 1971 Area D was excavated only north of Wall D.1:4.[2] In 1973 Area D was expanded south of Square D.3 by opening Square D.4 to link the acropolis access route with the proposed roadway in Area B.

Reported here are the results of the 1973 excavations in all squares of Area D except the new Square D.4 (assigned to the Area B supervisor[3] because it was presumably more clearly associated stratigraphically with Area B than with Area D). For lack of space the present report, summarizing a 37-page unpublished report, gives principally the most important 1973 data. In the context of the previous seasons' results it offers a comprehensive interpretation of Area D through at least 12 strata (several subdivided).[4] The only constant architectural

[1] On the results of the 1968 season, see *AUSS,* 7 (1969): 97-222 (henceforth referred to as "Heshbon 1968"). For Area D specifically, see P. A. Bird, "Heshbon 1968: Area D," pp. 165-217.

[2] On the results of the 1971 season, see *AUSS,* 11 (1973): 1-144 (henceforth referred to as "Heshbon 1971"). For Area D specifically, see L. T. Geraty, "Heshbon 1971: Area D," pp. 89-112.

[3] For J. A. Sauer's report, see pp. 133-167.

[4] The dates given for each stratum are approximate. In addition to stratigraphic and other evidence from Area D, they are derived from literary and site-wide numismatic and ceramic evidence as cited by Sauer in *Heshbon Pottery 1971* (AUM 7; Berrien Springs, Mich., 1973).

feature in Area D (in at least 10 strata) was Wall D.1:4,[5] the acropolis perimeter wall. It effectively divided the horizontal northern sector, a part of the acropolis proper, from the sloping southern sector, part of an approach to the acropolis.

### Stratum 1: Modern (A.D. 1917-1968)

A few fence walls on topsoil and some small objects, but no major architecture, were attributed to the Modern resettlement of Ḥesbân.[6] Ceramic and numismatic evidence indicated a stratigraphic gap between Strata 1 and 2. The latest attested pottery was Ayyūbid/Mamlūk, and the latest coins came from the rule of Az̤-Z̤āhir Barḳūḳ, A.D. 1382-1399.[7]

### Stratum 2: Mamlūk (14th/15th Centuries A.D.)

Area D's second stratum represented a period of decay. The gateway through Wall D.1:4a, the southern entrance to the acropolis for at least 1,000 years, was blocked by Wall D.1:9. The vaulted room in Squares D.1 and 6, built in Stratum 3, fell into ruin, and on the eastern slope of this ruin small terraces[8] were built, perhaps for horticultural purposes. If so, water was probably (on numismatic evidence) still drawn from Cistern D.5:5.[9] Either the sector south of Wall D.1:4 was then unoccupied or all traces of it eroded away during the long post-Stratum 2 gap.

### Stratum 3: Mamlūk (14th Century A.D.)

Structures and soil layers in Stratum 3 reflect the last main occupation period in Area D (cf. Fig 6). Wall D.1:4 was rebuilt (Phase B) with a new double gateway[10] leading, on the north, to an earth courtyard (D.1:39=D.5:7), in which Cistern D.5:5 saw

[5] Although Cisterns D.5:5 and D.6:33 were probably used during the time of most strata, their mouths underwent changing construction.

[6] See Sauer, "Heshbon 1971," p. 35, and references there.

[7] A. Terian, "Heshbon 1971 Coins," AUSS, 12 (1974): 40, 41. This statement is accurate if Coin No. 215 is taken as Seljuk of Rum rather than early Ottoman.

[8] Fully described in Geraty, "Heshbon 1971," pp. 104, 105.

[9] For plan, sections, and photograph, see "Heshbon 1971," Fig. 5 (p. 96), and Pl. IX:B.

[10] See Bird, "Heshbon 1968," pp. 197, 202, 203, and Pl. XX:A.

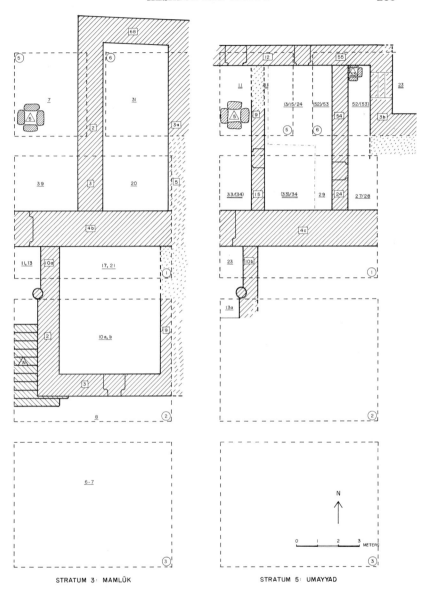

STRATUM 3: MAMLŪK                    STRATUM 5: UMAYYAD

**Fig. 6.** Schematic plans of Area D showing relationship of principal loci in the Mamlūk and Umayyad strata. Key: Circled numerals refer to Square designations, boxed numerals to walls, underlined numerals to surfaces, while numerals enclosed in triangles are either cisterns or stairways.

continued use. Immediately to the east, deep foundations were dug for three walls (west, D.1:3=D.5:2; north, D.6:68; east, D.1:5=D.6:3a) of a 6.00 x 9.00 m. vaulted room ca. 2.00 m. high, butted up against Wall D.1:4b. The room, excavated in 1968[11] and 1971,[12] had a probable south window[13] and a series of matching Ayyūbid/Mamlūk earth (occupational) and plaster layers; it could be dated to ca. A.D. 1380 at the latest by coins in Cistern D.6:33[14] sealed by the original floor (D.1:20=D.6:31).[15] Of its northern wall (D.6:68), excavated in 1973, only the bottom two courses remained, with no certain evidence of a doorway. The room could have been open to the north—with no doorway as such—if it belonged to a caravanserai-type complex around a courtyard within the acropolis, in Area A. In any case, it contained evidence for domestic usage.

The new gateway through Wall D.1:4b (partly in the west balk) mentioned above, went through two phases, perhaps corresponding to the two phases (D.1:11, 13) of a plaster-floored porch adjoining it to the south. This porch and Stairway D.2:7a leading up to it from the south were flanked on the east by a retaining wall (D.1:10a=D.2:12)[16] separating them from the 5.00 x 6.00 m. courtyard lying at the level from which Stair D.2:7a rose (on exterior Surface D.2:8=D.3:6/7). This southern approach to the acropolis—stairs, porch, and gateway—was but the last rebuilding of a basic structure originating no later than the Early Byzantine period (Stratum 7). This courtyard was bounded on the west by retaining Wall D.1:10a=D.2:2, on the north by Wall D.1:4, on the east by Wall D.2:9, and on the south by Wall

[11] Ibid., pp. 197-202.

[12] Geraty, "Heshbon 1971," pp. 99-101.

[13] Bird, "Heshbon 1968," pp. 201, 202.

[14] See Terian, "Heshbon 1971 Coins," p. 40; discussed also in Sauer, Heshbon Pottery 1971, pp. 57, 58.

[15] For a north section drawing through this room, see Geraty, "Heshbon 1971," Fig. 4 (p. 90).

[16] "Heshbon 1968," Pl. XX:B.

D.2:3, which had a two-phase threshold corresponding to the original level (D.1:21=D.2:10b) and resurfacing (D.1:17= D.2:10a) of the courtyard (so called for lack of evidence of roofing, though some evidence of domestic activity was found in 1968). Despite the good condition of the floor, its suggested use as a parking place for horses outside the acropolis became reasonable after two crescent-shaped iron horseshoes were found on Surface D.1:17.[17] In any case, Stratum 3 appeared to be the innovative one within the period of the Ayyūbid/Mamlūk occupation of Area D.[18]

### Stratum 4: Ayyūbid/Mamlūk (13/14th Centuries A.D.)

Apparently no significant Ayyūbid/Mamlūk construction took place in Area D prior to Stratum 3. Wall D.1:4c of Stratum 4 was in disrepair, though its old gateway (probably partly buried) opened on the acropolis, where Cisterns D.5:5 and D.6:33 were in use.[19] The latter was accessible also from the east through Threshold 1 of Wall D.6:3b, the Byzantine wall underlying the eastern wall of the vaulted room of Stratum 3. Surrounding these cistern mouths, north of Wall D.1:4, were soil surfaces (D.1:12 and 22, D.5:8, and D.6:49) accumulated during the long post-Stratum 5 gap. Contemporary soil layers south of Wall D.1:4 were not found, because of erosion or the extensive pits dug in Squares D.2 and 3 prior to the courtyard construction of Stratum 3. Thus Stratum 4 was chiefly what the earliest Ayyūbid/Mamlūk settlers found in Area D and used without significant structural changes.

The absence of stratification, pottery, or coins from the 450 years between Strata 4 and 5 in Area D, confirmed by sitewide negative evidence, points to a long abandonment of Tell Ḥesbân.

[17] Bird, "Heshbon 1968," pp. 208, 209.

[18] A stone-for-stone plan of Squares D.1 and 2 in Stratum 3 appeared in "Heshbon 1968," Fig. 10 (opposite p. 176).

[19] For the coin evidence, cf. footnote 14.

## Stratum 5: Umayyad (A.D. 640-750)

Stratum 5 was essentially a continuation of Late Byzantine
Stratum 6, but with a major new adaptation of the floor space
north of Wall D.1:4 (see Fig. 6).[20] Already present between that
wall and Wall D.5:12=D.6:55 to the north (the southern exterior
Byzantine church wall), was the fine flagstone floor of Courtyard
D.1:33/34=D.5:11 of Stratum 6. This floor had undoubtedly
extended eastward to boundary Wall D.6:56a until its northeast
quadrant had been robbed out in the Byzantine or the Early
Umayyad period. Perhaps at this time the huge architraves had
fallen on contemporary surfaces before the entrances through
Walls D.1:4c and D.6:56a, as well as other large and small architectural fragments—many of which were incorporated in the
building of Stratum 5. These Umayyad builders, since they used
*in situ* the remains of Stratum 6, were likely not responsible for the
preceding destruction. More probably it was the Persians who are
known to have destroyed many Palestinian Christian churches in
A.D. 614. If so, the Umayyad builders would then have patched
up Floor D.1:33/34=D.5:11 (burying numerous Byzantine glass
fragments in the process). For lack of pavers (as in the northeast
quadrant) they would have leveled up the courtyard with Soil
Layer D.5:13/15/24=D.6:52/53=D.1:27/28/29.[21] On this flag-
stone/packed-earth courtyard, between Cisterns D.5:5 and D.6:33,
and butting up against the acropolis perimeter wall on the south
and the south wall of the church on the north, they built Walls
D.1:15=D.5:9 (west) and D.1:24=D.6:54 (east), forming a
3.50 x 7.00 m. room with a north entrance and west and east
exits to the cisterns. Fragments of marble slabs (screens?) in both
new walls may have come from the Area A church. The room's
function was unknown, though evidence for domestic use was

[20] See also "Heshbon 1968," Fig. 9 (p. 171), a stone-for-stone plan of
Stratum 5 in Square D.1 (except for the Strata 6/7 threshold).

[21] For a photograph of how the courtyard may have looked after the floor
patching job but before the leveling up process, see "Heshbon 1971," Pl. IX:A
(disregard later Stratum 3 wall at upper left).

found on exterior Surface D.1:27/28, which gave access both to
Cistern D.6:33 and (through Wall D.6:3b's narrow doorway) to
reused tessellated Floor D.6:23.

Wall D.1:4c's gateway was provided with a new threshold,
raised probably to match the resurfaced Porch D.1:23=D.2:13a
on the south. This porch, with Wall D.1:10b on the east, may have
had its own stairs (not preserved), but was more likely associated
with use of the series of Early Byzantine stairs of Stratum 7. All
further traces of Stratum 5 south of Wall D.1:4 were apparently
eroded during the post-Stratum 5 gap.

### Stratum 6: Late Byzantine (A.D. 491-640)

Stratum 6 was closely related architecturally to Strata 5 and 7
(see Fig. 7). It was apparently a transition between the original
construction of the Christian church in Area A and its final alteration. In Stratum 7 the space between Walls D.1:4 on the south
and D.5:12=D.6:55 on the north had been divided into three
sectors, each with its own surface. The builders of Stratum 6
decided to divide this space into only two and to pave with flagstones the western sector lying between the two doorways in Walls
D.1:4 and D.5:12=D.6:55; but at least three preliminary changes
were needed: First, east-west Wall D.5:27=D.6:70, about
midway between Walls D.1:4 and D.5:12=D.6:55, had to be
dismantled before paving the courtyard (unless it was only one
course high and served as a mosaic border, like similar Wall
D.6:3c). Second, for the courtyard's eastern border, Wall D.6:56a
had to be built over Wall D.6:56b in the north and extended south
to Wall D.1:4 over limestone-tiled Floor D.1:41. Third, from an
existing downspout emptying into Catch Basin D.5:31 at the
western juncture of Walls D.5:12=D.6:55 and D.6:56, a new
water channel (D.6:63) replacing one (D.5:20) formerly leading
to Cistern D.5:5, was built in a reverse S curve eastward into
Cistern D.6:63 (cf. Pl. VI:B). The old Channel D.5:20 possibly
belonged to an earlier phase of Stratum 6, but more probably

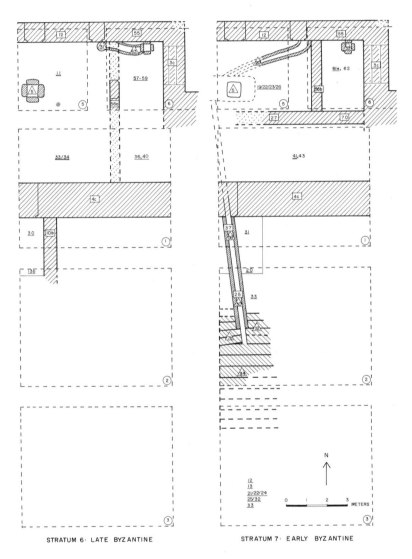

STRATUM 6: LATE BYZANTINE            STRATUM 7: EARLY BYZANTINE

Fig. 7. Schematic plans of Area D showing relationship of principal loci in the Late and Early Byzantine strata. Key: Circled numerals refer to Square designations, boxed numerals to walls, underlined numerals to surfaces, numerals with a double underlining refer to pavements or floors, while numerals enclosed in triangles are either cisterns or stairways.

to Stratum 7. The above three changes enabled Stratum 6 builders to pave with giant flagstones (many 1.00 x .50 m.) the entire Courtyard D.1:33/34=D.5:11 between Walls D.1:4, D.5:12= D.6:55, and D.6:56a. This last wall provided an exit leading to Cistern D.6:33 and to associated soil Surfaces D.6:57-59=D.1:36, 40, probably an occupational build-up on Surface D.6:51a=D.1: 41. Thence a flight of 2.00-m.-long steps led through Wall D.6:3c to reach tessellated Floor D.6:23, undoubtedly reused from Stratum 7.

The Stratum 7 gateway in Wall D.1:4c continued in use apparently unaltered. Outside its threshold, the porch at the head of the Stratum 7 stair was resurfaced (D.1:30=D.2:13b) and narrowed by a new boundary/retaining wall (D.1:10b). Since no other stairs were found, Stratum 6 seemed to have reused the Stratum 7 stairway(s). No Stratum 6 structures or soil layers were found south of Wall D.1:4c and east of the D.2 stairway complex; they must have been lost by pitting or erosion during the post-Stratum 5 gap. The Stratum 6 finds in Area D most likely came from a major remodeling of the church and its related structures.

## Stratum 7: Early Byzantine (A.D. 324-491)

Stratum 7 represented a radical alteration of the acropolis and its southern approach in Area D (see Fig. 7), especially north of Wall D.1:4. The natural (?) entrance to Cistern D.5:5 may have been vaulted at this time,[22] while the neck of Cistern D.6:33 was enclosed by four rectangular stones placed stretcher-style around the mouth (instead of the header-style eight-stone arrangement of the earlier strata). The changes seemed to be connected with the building of a basilica-type Christian church on the acropolis. All excavated parts of this church lay in Area A, however, except its southern exterior Wall D.5:12=D.6:55 and related features. The 8.00 m. length of this wall excavated in Area D, six courses

[22] See "Heshbon 1971," Pl. IX:B.

high and two rows thick, appeared in three structural phases: Phase C, the bottom two courses, of large, rough field stones set on bedrock, probably foundational, conceivably the remnant of an earlier wall; Phase B, the first well-dressed course; then Phase A, the top three preserved courses, of slightly narrower stones. In the balk between Squares D.5 and 6, the lowest course of the upper phase served as a threshold, perhaps for a minor entrance to the south aisle of the church (as opposed to the wider entrance ca. 2.50 m. west). Where Wall D.6:55 crossed over Cistern D.6:33, next to the cistern neck, it contained a blocked-in structural arch 1.75 m. high, spanning 2.75 m. at its base. The arch undoubtedly served to spread the weight of the church's structure rather than rest it on the cistern ceiling. Wall D.5:12= D.6:55 was not dismantled but the adjoining soil layers, including Foundation Trench D.6:76, all the way to its bedrock base were Early Byzantine.

Probably bonded to Wall D.6:55 at its eastern end was Wall D.6:3c, running south 2.50 m. to abut Wall D.6:19c, which ran east and out of Square D.6. Accommodated to these latter two walls (also to an unexcavated wall ca. .75 m. east of the east balk) was tessellated Floor D.6:23; apparently this was a vestry just south of the apse.[23] Wall D.6:3c contained a flight of 2.00-m.-long steps leading up to the location of Cistern D.6:33. At this level the Stratum 7 builders divided the space between the acropolis perimeter wall and the southern exterior church wall into three sectors by constructing two new walls in or close to the balks of Squares D.1, 5, and 6. Wall D.6:70=D.5:27, one course high, one row thick, of well-dressed, tightly-fitting stones all set as headers, was founded on the Late Roman Surface D.1:44= D.6:69 of Stratum 8 and ran east-west in the balk separating Square D.1 from Squares D.5 and 6; though its purpose was unclear, it separated contemporary and similar Floor D.6:61a to the northeast and Floor D.1:41 to the south. Running from

[23] For a fuller description and photographs, see Geraty, "Heshbon 1971," pp. 105, 106, and Pl. X:A, B.

this wall to the church's south wall (D.5:12=D.6:55) just east of the west balk of Square D.6, was Wall D.6:56b, two rows thick but one course high, obviously a different and earlier phase of Wall D.6:56a. Both these new walls were bonded with rough, clayey red soil that adhered to the sides of the stones. As mentioned, Surface D.6:61a was the floor for this northeast sector; yellowish, clayey, and extremely hard in places, it lay over D.6:62, a crumbly, rust-colored layer. This floor and its make-up corresponded in texture and level to D.1:41, the well preserved dolomitic limestone tile floor with its reddish mortar base (D.1:43) south of Wall D.6:70=D.5:27.[24]

The third sector created by the two new walls (D.6:70=D.5:27 and D.6:56b) corresponded to the space of our Square D.5 and its east balk. In Stratum 6 the western half of this sector was covered by Flagstone Floor D.5:11 which, on the request of the national Department of Antiquities, was not dismantled; here the underlying earlier strata were not excavated. Yet certain features can be described: The downspout and predecessor of Catch Basin D.5:31 mentioned above (Stratum 6), evidently part of the church's original construction in Stratum 7, emptied into .40-m.-deep Channel D.5:20, stone lined and carefully cemented, which would have carried rain water to Cistern D.5:5 (see Pl. VI:B). Whether it was built covered or open was not learned. Adjoining both channel walls and covering the rest of the sector was a yellowish-green, clayey surface (D.5:19/22/ 23/26)—very similar in texture and certainly contemporary with

---

[24] See the fuller description in Geraty, "Heshbon 1971," pp. 92, 93. In 1971, Coin No. 168, a Roman *aes* IV type of the 4th-5th centuries A.D., was found in Floor D.1:41, agreeing well with its attribution to Stratum 7 (Terian, "Heshbon 1971 Coins," p. 35, n. 3). In 1973, Coin (Object Registry) No. 1643, dated to the reign of Justinian I (A.D. 527-565), was recorded as found in mint condition in D.1:43 next to wall D.6:70 (Terian, "Heshbon 1973 Coins," *AUSS,* forthcoming). Obviously this presented a problem; on stratigraphic and ceramic grounds, these walls and associated soil layers could not be attributed to Stratum 6 as required by the Justinian coin. It was therefore interpreted as intrusive, especially since it came from balk removal directly under the projected course of Stratum 6 Wall D.6:56a.

floor Surfaces D.6:61a and D.1:41 already described. Before the laying of this floor the mouth of Cistern D.5:5, probably an enlarged and deepened natural cave (entered laterally from the east), was altered. Probably the Stratum 7 builders walled up the natural cave entrance with Wall D.6:56c which was set further to the west than Walls D.6:56a and b, then covering the entire mouth with a vaulted ceiling of cut stones, left only the vertical entrance at the top.[25] Where probed, all these features were dated Early Byzantine.

In Stratum 7, two (preserved) courses of finely cut and fitted limestone blocks were added to the giant field stones of Wall D.1:4d.[26] The gateway of this new phase (Wall D.1:4c), a fine example of the mason's skill, was maintained, reused and rebuilt through all later strata.[27] To the south, outside the gate, plastered Surface D.1:31=D.2:20 formed a kind of porch at the head of a stairway, or a series of stairways, running down further to the south—presumably (though the robbed-out lower stairs had to be projected) until they met a series of superimposed plaster and soil layers in the southwestern quadrant of Square D.3 which could clearly be related to similar soil layers in Square B.3 described in 1971.[28] There the layers were interpreted as resurfacings of an Early Roman-Early Byzantine roadway that approached the *tell* from either west or south. Though Layer D.3:12 could be identified with Layer B.3:2 (Area B, Stratum 5), and Layer D.3:13 with Layer B.3:3 (Area B, Stratum 6), the underlying layers of Square D.3 were not as readily identifiable with those of Square B.3. In a general way, however, the following loci could be correlated: Layer D.3:21/22/24[29] with Layers B.3:5-

[25] See "Heshbon 1971," Pl. IX:B.

[26] More fully described in Bird, "Heshbon 1968," pp. 170, 175, 176, and Fig. 9, p. 171 (Wall D.1:4c only; construction to the left belongs to later strata).

[27] *Ibid.*, p. 177.

[28] Sauer, "Heshbon 1971," pp. 48-57.

[29] Locus D.3:24 contained Coin (Object Registry) No. 1525, dated to the reign of Valentinian II (A.D. 375-392) by Terian, "Heshbon 1973 Coins," *AUSS*, forthcoming.

21 (Area B, Stratum 7); Layer D.3:25/32 with Layers B.3:22-23
(Area B, Stratum 8); and Layer D.3:33 (an extensive Early Byzantine yellowish *huwwar* layer with many plaster fragments)
with Layers B.3:24-25 (Area B, Stratum 9). The contemporary
surfaces east of the stairway/roadway sector in Squares D.2 and 3
were not recovered, probably because of erosion or pitting.

Details of stairway reconstruction in Square D.2 were difficult
to recover, primarily because the stratigraphy was so complex;
but after meticulous work the following interpretation became
clear: South of Wall D.1:4c, under Porch D.1:31=D.2:20, lay
"Wall" D.1:37=D.2:25 (first designated D.2:2b in 1968). Its
exposed 5.80 m. length, one course high, one row wide, when
traced diagonally from just below the D.1:4c gateway to the
center of the Square D.2 stairway complex, proved to be rather
the covering stones for well-constructed Water Channel D.1:58=
D.2:30 (cf. Pl. VIII:A for a view of this and other features discussed below). The channel was narrower in the north as it
passed through Wall D.1:4, under the threshold, probably leading from Cistern D.5:5; on stratigraphic evidence the channel
formed part of the Stratum 7 D.1:4c gateway. Further, its central
portion, founded on plaster Surface D.2:33 (overlying Late
Roman loci), cut Late Roman Stairway D.2:32, and its southern
end passed off the highest visible course of stone Stair D.2:34
(Early Byzantine, see below).

Already in 1968 at least three phases in this stairway complex
were noted, the latest (D.2:7a) dated Ayyūbid/Mamlūk.[30] In
1973 three further stairs (besides D.2:7a) were identified,
dismantled, and dated. The latest was Stair D.2:7b whose steps
were accommodated and even bonded to the western side of the
central portion of Channel D.1:58=D.2:30 and aligned to its
angle, and thus contemporary with it. The second stair identified
was D.2:34 (noted merely as "sub-7" in 1968), the lowest of
all of them. Its steps were of rectangular stones laid end to end

[30] Bird, "Heshbon 1968," pp. 209, 210.

lengthwise in three staggered rows. It obviously superseded, and perhaps repaired, the third stairway, Late Roman Stair D.2:32 (of Stratum 8; see below)—at least on the south end. Stratigraphically and ceramically dated Early Byzantine Stair D.2:34 could have come from an earlier phase in Stratum 7 than Channel D.1:58=D.2:30, for instance.

### Stratum 8: Late Roman (A.D. 193?-324) [31]

Stratum 8 represented another radical change in the acropolis and its southern access route in Area D, second only to what followed in Stratum 7 (see Fig. 8). Indicative of major building north of Wall D.1:4d was a 1.25 m. deep rubble fill with rocks, gravel, loose dirt, air pockets, and 32 pails of sherds from a 3.00 x 3.00 m. sector alone. A similar fill, also ceramically dated Late Roman, was found north of Wall D.6:19d to the northeast of Square D.1. Was this rubble fill to level the sector over the newly constructed vaulted ceiling over Cistern D.5:5 as was suggested in 1971,[32] or was it (as now seems more likely) a part of a larger operation turning the acropolis summit into a platform for an important public building? Beaten Surface D.1:44=D.6:69 covered this fill and surrounded the neck of Cistern D.6:33 (with its header, or petal, arrangement of curb stones probably built in Stratum 10). Features of Stratum 8 along the west balks of Squares D.1 and 5, including the mouth of Cistern D.5:5, were not uncovered since they lay below the unexcavated Stratum 6 flagstone floor.

Wall D.1:4d, the bottom four (irregular) courses of rough field boulders chinked with smaller stones that underlay the Stratum 7 rebuild, must date from Stratum 10 at the latest; their use in Stratum 8 was not clear since any higher courses were apparently destroyed in the Early Byzantine rebuild. Only south of Early Roman Wall D.2:21/26 were Stratum 8 loci again

[31] This chronological division at A.D. 193 for the two Late Roman strata in Area D rests on Sauer's suggestion for contemporary Stratum 10 in Area B; see his *Heshbon Pottery 1971,* p. 29.

[32] Geraty, "Heshbon 1971," p. 111.

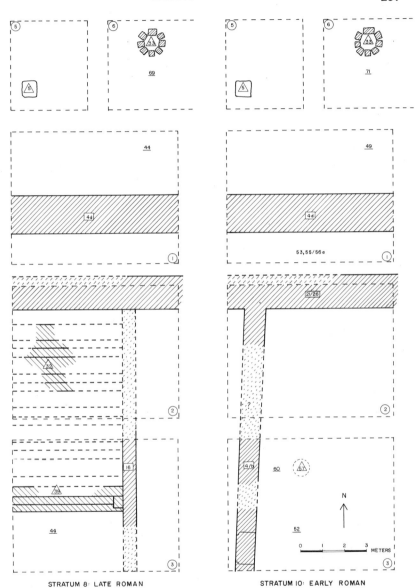

STRATUM 8: LATE ROMAN

STRATUM 10: EARLY ROMAN

Fig. 8. Schematic plans of Area D showing relationship of principal loci in the Late and Early Roman strata. Key: Circled numerals refer to Square designations, boxed numerals to walls, underlined numerals to surfaces, while numerals enclosed in triangles are either cisterns or stairways.

found, associated with the remnants of Stairway D.2:32 (mentioned above). This stair had a central level strip of stone paving/terracing, visible even before the removal of Stair D.2:34, with three low shallow steps to the north (cf. Pl. VIII:A) and two more steps to the south. The stones were laid crosswise, their long sides together, with a consistent tread of .20 m. Stairway D.2:32 was clearly more extensive than the six preserved courses since it had certainly been robbed away to the north, east, and south. The extensive make-up (nearly 2.00 m. deep) for D.2:32 (D.2:35, 36, 40 and 43) was filled with characteristic architectural fragments and many Late Roman sherds.[33] This whole build-up for the Stratum 8 stairway complex was laid up against Wall D.2:21/26 to the north and presumably originally went on over it to Wall D.1:4d. The southward extension of D.2:32 had been robbed away; but in the center of Square D.3, ca. 4 m. to the south, were found three preserved courses of Stairway D.3:39, of identical construction; its profile, when computed from the tread and depth and projected upward, matched and would have met (if the intervening steps had not been robbed away) this Stairway D.2:32. The three steps of the broad Stair D.3:39 extended east out of the west balk ca. 5.20 m. to north-south Wall D.3:16, its eastern boundary (cf. Pl. VII:A)—a large, apparently one-row wide wall founded on bedrock, probably into both north and south balks, but badly destroyed in its upper courses (perhaps originally faced with finished slabs covering its boulder-and-chink-stone construction). Where the bottom step met Wall D.3:16, it was surmounted by a beveled cornerstone. In the debris just above it another unique architectural member was found, of the dimensions and cut of an ideal corresponding capital for a balustrade beginning at the beveled cornerstone and running north up the steps along Wall D.3:16 (Pl. VII:B). Under and

[33] This make-up included Coin (Object Registry) No. 1647, dated to the reign of Trajan (A.D. 98-117), according to Terian, "Heshbon 1973 Coins," *AUSS*, forthcoming; it was obviously earlier than the dominant Late Roman pottery found there.

north of Stair D.3:39 was an extensive 2.00 m. deep Late Roman fill containing characteristic architectural fragments similar to those in the make-up for Stairway D.2:32. Thus a number of facts argue that Stairs D.2:32 and D.2:39 were one. Built with such grand proportions, it must have led to an important public building on the acropolis—possibly the predecessor(s) of the Byzantine Church in Area A. This stairway was approached from the south by a series of superimposed hard *huwwar*-surfaced layers, the original probably being Surface D.3:44. Further excavation may connect these with the Area B roadway series. Square D.3 remained unexcavated east of Wall D.3:16.

### *Stratum 9: Late Roman* (A.D. *135-193?*)[34]

The only good evidence for a pre-Stratum 8 Late Roman stratum was found in Square D.3. Immediately under Stair D.3:39 and its associated surfaces, and running the full 6.00 m. along the west balk, were found three courses of Wall D.3:47 (cf. Pl. VII:A). The upper preserved courses (D.3:47a) included a threshold and doorway in the south portion, opening in to the east, and part of a doorway near the north balk. Associated with this phase of the wall (only south of Steps D.3:39) was a hard brown earth Surface D.3:49, laid up to the level of the threshold stone itself and thus presumably the floor of a Late Roman building that was destroyed by the builders of Stratum 8.

### *Stratum 10: Early Roman (63* B.C.-A.D. *135)*

The evidence from 1973 indicated that Stratum 10, too, was an innovative one, but until further excavation takes place, particularly in Squares D.2 and 3, conclusions must remain tentative (see Fig. 8.). North of Wall D.1:4d the picture was very similar to Stratum 8: Early Roman Surface D.1:49= D.6:44=D.6:71, just above bedrock, seemed to be associated with the new header-type construction around the mouth of

---

[34] For A.D. 193 see Sauer, *Heshbon Pottery 1971*, p. 29.

Cistern D.6:33. The latter was connected by a subterranean channel to interconnected Cisterns D.6:47 and 48 (last used in Stratum 10) in a manner already described in 1971.[35]

The construction date of Wall D.1:4d was an interesting puzzle. In 1971, since the earliest soil layers on bedrock north of it were Early Roman, it was then thought to be Early Roman also.[36] But in 1973, below clear Early Roman Soil Layers D.1:53, 55/56a (up against the south face of Wall D.1:4d), a series of soil layers 1.50 m. deep to bedrock (D.1:56 Hell., 59, and 60) produced 37 (mostly full) pails of only Late Hellenistic and Iron II sherds! There were only two alternatives: either (a) D.1:4d was a Roman wall, with Roman surfaces north of it and a Roman fill of Hellenistic material south of it, *or* (b) it was a Hellenistic wall with Hellenistic build-up on both faces originally, with the Hellenistic remains to the north cleared away to bedrock when the wall was rebuilt by the Romans during their restructuring of the acropolis. Against hypothesis (a): There were no tip lines or other evidence that the Hellenistic layers were a Roman fill (unless the many scattered *ṭabun* fragments are so considered), nor any tell-tale Roman sherds; further, why would fill be dumped *outside* a perimeter wall? Only if used in building a casemate-type fortification using Wall D.2:21/26 as the outside or retaining wall. In favor of (a): This latter wall, running the full length of, and partially in, D.2's north balk was three rows thick, slanting to the north as it rose from a lower bedrock shelf than that on which Wall D.1:4d stood. Its inner, northern face was battered against the Early Roman and Hellenistic layers just described (cf. Pl. VIII: B); the outer, southern face, built of smaller stones with traces of cement, was laid against the central row as though to strengthen it. The dismantled portion of each row dated Early Roman. Whether contemporary with or later than Wall D.1:4d, this Stratum 10 wall was clearly a retaining wall outside the huge acropolis perimeter wall. Its upper courses were apparently

[35] Geraty, "Heshbon 1971," pp. 107, 108, and Fig. 6 (p. 102).
[36] *Ibid.*, p. 94.

cut away on the west for Channel D.2:30=D.1:58 of Stratum 7 and were robbed away on the east by a huge Ayyūbid/Mamlūk pit. Near the west balk and bonded to the south face of Wall D.2:21 was a wall two rows thick, five courses high, running south ca. 2.00 m., then robbed away. Only future excavation will show whether it continued south to Stratum 10 Wall D.3:47b, the lower phase of Stratum 9 Wall D.3:47a. Associated with the former was the earliest surface (D.3:52/60) extending throughout the excavated portions of Square D.3. In the southwest quadrant, Surface D.3:52 covered huge chunks of bedrock (some of which may once have covered caves but were) now tipped at various angles, perhaps by an earthquake during the Early Roman period;[37] and in the northwest quadrant, Surface D.3:60 covered a stone slab wall (D.3:63) that protected the mouth of unexcavated Cistern D.3:57. Any Stratum 10 remains in the eastern parts of Squares D.2 and 3 await further excavation.

### Stratum 11: Late Hellenistic (198-63 B.C.)

Only bits and pieces of a Hellenistic stratum could be put together—because of both ancient destruction and our unfinished excavation. North of Wall D.1:4 most of the cisterns probably either existed or were constructed during the period of Stratum 11. In Square D.6, one surface (D.6:72) and one possible wall (D.6:75) were found. The possible Hellenistic data for Wall D.1:4d has been discussed above. On the narrow bedrock shelf south of Wall D.1:4d, a giant boulder resting on a one-row thick wall at first blocked the entrance to Cave D.1:63 which was later found to have been carved out of bedrock and plastered. Sherds in its first soil layer were Hellenistic; discovery of its full extent and function awaits futher excavation.

### Stratum 12: Iron Age

No pre-Hellenistic architectural evidence was found in Area D,

[37] See Sauer, "Heshbon 1971," p. 50.

though abundant Iron Age sherds (primarily 7th/6th centuries B.C.) in mixed loci attested an occupation in the vicinity.

In conclusion, it is interesting to note that from the Ayyūbid/ Mamlūk Stratum 1 back to at least the Early Byzantine Stratum 7, most of our evidence lay north of Wall D.1:4, perhaps because the acropolis approach was less important in those periods, but more likely because a slope suffers erosion of its top layers, since from Early Byzantine Stratum 7 back at least to Early Roman Stratum 10 we found more extensive remains south of Wall D.1:4.

# NECROPOLIS AREA F

DEWEY M. BEEGLE

Wesley Theological Seminary, Washington, D.C.

The eight tombs excavated were all in the Necropolis Area F, about 660 meters southwest of the acropolis (see Fig. 1). Five were clustered to the north and northwest of the swinging-door Tomb F.5 (see Fig. 9), and the other three about 105 meters southwest of it.

Of the two basic tomb types, the more common was the *vertical-shaft tomb*. The simpler form of this was a rectangular shaft cut vertically into the limestone, much like an ordinary grave today. The more complex form had a deep shaft which widened out near the bottom on each long side into a small arcosolium-like alcove, with a curved or arched ceiling. A rectangular grave was cut into the floor of each alcove. The upper part of the shaft was cut out a little wider. On the ledge thus formed, stone slabs were laid and covered with earth to ground level. The second basic type was the *chamber tomb with loculi*. Entrance was through a doorway and down steps leading into a main chamber with a square, shallow central pit. The graves consisted of a number of loculi, shafts cut horizontally into three walls at floor level and extending lengthwise at right angles to the walls.

In order to gain as accurate a picture as possible of the history of each tomb, great care was taken to excavate the earth fill stratigraphically. Then the fill was sifted locus by locus for pottery, objects, and bones.

At the beginning of the season, in preparation for continuing the work of 1971, Philip Hammond and his University of Utah team conducted magnetometer and resistivity tests in a sector 10 x 30 m., running northeast to southwest, just to the west of

Tomb F.5. The magnetometer survey results were not useful, but the resistivity chart indicated three or four likely tomb locations.

*Tombs F.11a and F.11b.*—One of the best prospects for finding other tombs was a sector northwest of Tomb F.5. Moving the 1971 dump north of this tomb revealed two vertical shafts, c. 50 m. deep, to bedrock. The dominant and latest pottery in each was Byzantine. The absence of bones indicated that the shafts were never used as graves, or were thoroughly cleaned out before filling.

*Tomb F.12.*—During excavation near the bottom of Tomb F.11a, hollow sounds indicated a chamber of some sort underneath. When a probe was made from the ground surface north of F.11a, a vertical-shaft Tomb F.12 was uncovered (see Fig. 9), filled with two separate Byzantine layers of soil (with bone fragments) sealing both graves. It is possible that during the Byzantine period the bones from F.11a and F.11b were deposited in F.12 to prevent further desecration and then covered with earth. Analysis of the thoroughly disarticulated bones in the graves indicated at least thirteen burials (nine adults and four children). One child's skull had the unusual feature of a vertical frontal suture. This could indicate a relationship to the family group buried in rolling-stone Tomb F.1, where six of the individuals (children and adults) had this rare cranial feature.

The pottery of both graves in F.12 was Byzantine or earlier. Four unreadable, lepton-like Roman coins were found. Their presence may reflect the Graeco-Roman custom of putting a coin in the mouth to pay Charon for ferrying the shade across the Styx. The bottom of the shaft, not used as a grave, yielded a crushed Late Roman lamp.

The coins and lamp date the construction and first use of the tomb in the late Roman period. After some reuse the tomb was robbed in either the very late Roman or the early Byzantine period. Later the two graves and the bottom of the shaft were filled; later yet, still within the Byzantine period, the tomb was

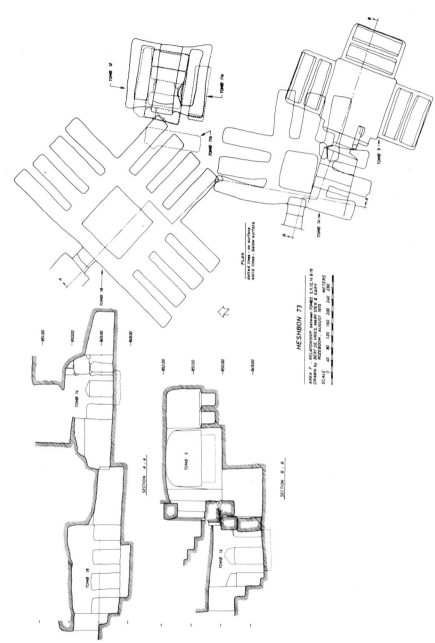

Fig. 9. Plan and sections of Tombs 5, 11, 12, 14 and 18.

filled completely. There was no indication of later reopening.

*Quarry F.13 and Tomb F.14.*—Under the dump north of Tomb
F.5 was found a north-south cut in the bedrock. A probe, labeled
F.13, turned out to be a rock-and-earth-filled quarry. However,
at its bottom was a breakthrough into a tomb chamber. This was
not far from Tomb F.5, where in the process of excavation in 1971
the floor in the northwest corner of the main chamber gave way
and revealed a small hollow chamber. Investigation in 1973 proved
it to be the loculus of another tomb. Its western end had been
blocked by large stones. Now a trench west of F.5 allowed location
of the entrance of this Tomb, F.14.

A stepped entranceway behind the large slab that sealed Tomb
F.14 was filled solid. At the left (north) of the entrance in the
main chamber was a mound of rocky fill. Layers of soil covered it
and filled the rest of the chamber up to the ceiling. Rodent tunnels, interlacing the fill, had caused some bone disturbance and
mixing of small sherds among the layers. The tomb had
three loculi each on the south, east, and north sides. These were
numbered counterclockwise from south to north. In the southeast
corner, Loculi 3 and 4 were blocked off by the large stones discovered from the breakthrough from Tomb F.5. Other stones
above them indicated that they were shoring to prevent the
collapse of the ceiling (Plate IX:A).

Underneath the fill on the north side of the chamber was a
thick layer of limestone from a massive collapse of the ceiling.
At the northeast corner of the chamber was the breakthrough
from the bottom of the Quarry F.13. Because the rocky fill in the
north half of the chamber continued up through the large hole
where the ceiling had once collapsed, excavation of Quarry F.13
was continued to the west to remove the fill over the tomb,
thereby lessening the danger of collapse while digging from
inside the tomb.

Two crushed, but restorable, two-handled Byzantine pots were
found under the fill in front of Loculus 2, and a whole carinated

Byzantine bowl was discovered under the limestone roof fall in front of Loculus 7. All the pottery of the pit[1] was Byzantine.

Loculi 1 and 2, filled with earth, contained no objects or bones; they were probably never used as graves. Fill from the main chamber spilled partly into Loculi 5-9, blocking the entrances.

Loculi 5-8 contained some bones, apparently one burial in each, but they were very friable. Further, they lay under slabs of limestone which had pulled loose from the ceilings of the loculi, apparently when the chamber ceiling collapsed. Loculus 9, which had no bones, had a small hole in the rear, opening into a loculus of another tomb.

Although loculus-type tombs were in style during the Early Roman period, exemplified by Tombs F.1, F.6, and F.8, excavated in 1971, the pottery evidence of Tomb F.14 quite conclusively dates its latest use in the Byzantine period. Tombs F.14 and F.6 are similar in size, in having nine loculi similarly oriented, and in having no stones sealing the loculi. One clear difference is that while Tomb F.6 had four lamp niches cut above the loculi, two with "Herodian" lamps still *in situ*, Tomb F.14 had no lamp niches, and no lamps or lamp fragments.

Assuming that Tomb F.14 was later than Tomb F.5, apparently one of the  workmen cutting out Loculus 3 of Tomb F.14 cut through the rock of the ceiling and into the chink stones and fill under the north end of the threshold stone of Tomb F.5. To prevent ceiling collapse, Loculus 3 was filled with earth, and then stone shoring was installed, thereby blocking access to Loculi 3 and 4. The fact that the east edge of the central pit was jogged slightly to the west, to clear the northernmost base-stone of the shoring, was taken as an indication that the shoring was constructed before the completion of the tomb.

[1] It should be noted that in the preliminary report on Area F in 1971, this type of pit was interpreted "as a sump, so that water seepage would not affect the burials" (*AUSS*, 11 [1973]: 115 and note 5). Since some of the *Ḥesbân* tomb loculi, especially in F.18, sloped away from the center and showed evidence of pools that had formed over the years, this interpretation may not be valid.

Evidently only one burial had been deposited in each of Loculi 5-8 when portions of the ceiling collapsed. It was difficult to ascertain whether robbers had gained entry before the collapse. Though this cave-in could have resulted from the work in the quarry above, the thickness of the roof fall suggested a severe tremor as the cause (perhaps the great earthquake of A.D. 365).

Not long after, the rocky fill was dumped into the tomb and the quarry above. The fill spilled into the northern loculi and formed a mound up to the ceiling break. In addition, earth layers were spread to the east and south of the rocky fill, some of them running into the loculi. Several centuries later, during the Ayyūbid/Mamlūk period, the tomb was discovered and filled to the ceiling. Then the entranceway was filled with earth, the stone slab sealed in place, and the antechamber filled in. Islamic concern to prevent desecration of the dead probably accounted for the care in filling and sealing the tomb.

*Tombs F.15 and F.17*—While the main crew was searching for the entrance to Tomb F.14, Helmi Musa, a Ta'amireh bedouin, was assigned to probe for other tombs. About 105 m. southwest of Tomb F.14 he uncovered vertical-shaft Tomb F.15 (Plate X:B). Probably because the north alcove had broken into the chamber of another tomb, no alcove was cut into the south face. The absence of bones or objects may indicate that the tomb was never used. The pottery in the fill, Byzantine and earlier, apparently dates the tomb in the Byzantine period.

A probe to the north of Tomb F.15 uncovered F.17, another vertical-shaft tomb (Pl. X:B). Both alcoves, thoroughly disturbed, yielded some bone fragments, but no objects. In the bottom of the shaft the lack of bones or objects indicated no burial. The pottery, none later than Byzantine in either the shaft or side graves, indicated Byzantine construction and use—earlier, however, than Tomb F.15. At least one individual was buried in each grave, but the thorough disturbance of the interior made it uncertain whether there were more than one. Tomb F.17, though designed like the Late Roman Tomb F.12, contained no lamps or lamp fragments.

*Tomb F.16.*—A few meters west of Tombs F.15 and F.17, at the base of the limestone terrace into which they were cut, Helmi Musa found vertical-shaft Tomb F.16, with a partly articulated skeleton in the east grave. Beneath were other skeletons, badly decomposed and mixed, which could not be accurately separated. Four unreadable coins were found. Bone analysis indicated five individuals in the east grave: the uppermost, a male, aged about 18 or 19, and, beneath him two adult males and two infants. The adults lay one on top of the other, separated by thin layers of earth.

The west grave contained the thoroughly disturbed bones of four adults, a child and an infant. One of the skulls had a vertical frontal suture like the child in Tomb F.12. Objects found included some jewelry, two whole glass vases, a Byzantine unguentarium, one Late Roman coin, and one (Object No. 1529) of Honorius, A.D. 395-423, early Byzantine. This legible coin and all the pottery indicated that the tomb was used in the Early Byzantine period and reused over a number of years.

The bottom of the shaft, without bones or objects, was probably never a grave.

*Tomb F.18.*—From the photographs and inspections made through the enlarged breakthrough from Loculus 9 in Tomb F.14 (Plate IX:B) it was possible to estimate the size of Tomb F.18. Our north-south probe trench intersected the rectangular ante-chamber with the sealing stone chinked in place. The stepped entranceway was packed with earth fill, but inside the chamber the fill, unlike that in Tomb F.14, sloped downward away from the entrance on all sides. Another mound of fill in the southeast corner had resulted from soil washed down through rodent tunnels in the ceiling. The back of Loculus 5 had some earth fill from the breakthrough from Loculus 9 of Tomb F.14. Over the eastern two-thirds of the chamber a thick layer of limestone roof fall separated the fill in the pit from the later layers above.

Loculus 1 held the bones of one adult, and one gold earring. The rest of the loculi (2-4) on the south side had no bones, but they may have been removed previously because a number of bones were found scattered along the south side of the pit. Loculus 3 had the largest collection of artifacts in the whole tomb (jewelry together with a number of whole pottery and glass vessels). Loculi 5-8, on the east side, had at least one adult burial in each grave, but two of them were buried with the feet toward the opening and the other two with the head toward the opening. Loculi 9-12, on the north side, sloped down away from the tomb center (Pl X:A), and Loculus 10 showed marks indicating that pools of water had formed at various times. Early burials in each loculus had been pushed to the rear in preparation for later burials, but such were not found in Loculi 9 and 12. The bone fragments in Loculus 9 did not comprise a complete skeleton. Either they were deposited in it from elsewhere in the tomb, or the skull and long bones had been removed. The practice of preserving the bones after the decay of the flesh was widespread during the Early Roman period in Palestine, but there was no clear evidence of this custom at Heshbon in Roman times. The infant bones in the Early Roman pot of Loculus 5 indicated concern, though the practice, if such it was, differed from usual patterns.

Tomb F.18 was well cut, with large loculi, most of which measured .50 x 1.00 x 2.00 m. The construction and first use of the tomb in the Early Roman period was quite evident from the three pots, two lamps, and six (Nabatean) coins, the latter from the reign of Aretas IV (9 B.C.-A.D. 40). Some of the glass vases found in the tomb may have come from this time. It was not possible to say how many of the loculi were used as graves in this period, since some of the pottery came from the main chamber. Moreover, some vessels may have been moved from one loculus to another. In general, however, it appeared that later users respected previous burials and artifacts (e.g. the infant bones in the Early Roman pot). Whether robbers entered the tomb in the Early Roman period was uncertain.

A cooking pot, cup, unguentarium, and lamps indicated clearly that the tomb was used again in the Late Roman period. Pottery in the upper layers of the pit showed that the ceiling fell in near the end of the Late Roman or early in the Byzantine period. The amount of limestone roof fall (plus that in some of the loculi) indicated a rather severe disturbance, though with less destruction than in Tomb F.14. It is quite possible that the severe earthquake of A.D. 365 was responsible for the collapse of the ceilings in both Tomb F.14 and Tomb F.18.

Some whole Byzantine vessels (two-handled pot and trumpet-base lamp) and single gold earrings in four separated loculi[2] indicated use also in the Byzantine period. When it was decided to abandon the tomb, earth fill in two layers, consistently Byzantine, was deposited, but whether at the same time is not certain. Locus F.18:6 contained some Umayyad and also Ayyūbid/Mamlūk sherds. These, if not intrusive, would indicate that both topmost layers were deposited between A.D. 1187 and 1441. There was no evidence that the tomb was reused during this period, though apparently someone discovered the tomb and made an inspection. Since the Byzantine fill did not cover the entrance completely, more was added. Unlike Tomb F.14, however, F.18 was not filled to the ceiling, but to the top of the inside entrance; the entranceway was packed solidly, the seal slab chinked into place, and the antechamber filled in. The tomb escaped subsequent disturbance until the official tomb excavators of 1973 came on the scene.

[2] The Amman Museum has similar earrings from Jerash dated 5th-6th century A.D. Since, as in Tomb F.18, only one earring was found with each burial, it was apparently a Byzantine custom to bury the deceased with a single earring.

# SOUNDINGS — AREA G

DEWEY M. BEEGLE

Wesley Theological Seminary, Washington, D.C.

*Square G.1.*—There was some evidence to indicate that early periods of ancient towns often saw occupation on the eastern side of the mound. Since no Squares had been opened on that side of *Tell Ḥesbân,* it seemed wise to have a sounding there to check the occupation sequence and compare it with data elsewhere on the mound. Square G.1, a probe 3.00 x 3.00 m., was opened on a terrace about 44 m. southeast of D.4 (see Fig. 1).

Considering the purpose of the sounding, the site selected presented some early inconveniences because of a series of super-imposed walls and cobblestone surfaces in the north half of the Square, all the way from topsoil to bedrock. Portions of these served as a built-in stairway for the excavating crew, but the limited working space south of them provided too little evidence to explain adequately their context and functions. The nature of a sounding did not permit sufficient scope to work out precisely the more complex relationships among the various loci. Neverthe-less, the broad outlines of the occupation history of this sector of Ḥesbân were clearly identified.

A number of layers and wall fragments attested a substantial Islamic settlement during the Ayyūbid/Mamlūk period. Though Byzantine occupation was clearly evident in other Areas of the mound, yet for some reason few Byzantine sherds and no clear-cut structures appeared in G.1. Late Roman was definitely repre-sented, but the peak of activity seems to have been in the Early Roman period. Fill with Iron I sherds covered bedrock (4.15 m. below topsoil) where it sloped downward in the southeast corner; but this layer was probably Hellenistic fill (from Iron Age occupation layers nearby) which served as a base for a lime-

213

stone surface. This evidence witnessed to the Hellenistic propensity to build on bedrock whenever possible.

In general, the evidence from G.1 indicated that the east side of the mound shared the same range and sequence as found in the four major Areas opened on the *tell*. Bone finds showed that throughout these various periods sheep, goats, and cattle were the animals most evidently basic to the life and economy of the people. The gaps in occupation were another story. When the Ayyūbid/Mamlūk occupation began, the mound had lain silent for several centuries after it had been a bustling hub of activity in the Transjordan plateau. Then after being active again for about two centuries, it fell into another long silence lasting almost five hundred years.

*Cistern G.2.*—Excavation of a cistern in *Ḥesbân* village was labeled G.2. Since its clearance would have taken many days, and two days' digging was unproductive, the project was discontinued.

*Sounding G.3*—Southwest of the acropolis, in the northwestern part of the village of *Ḥesbân*, were the ruins of an Islamic *Qasr*, "Castle." In order to date this substantial structure, soundings (1.50 x 2.50 m.) were opened inside and outside the south exterior wall and set perpendicular to a window ledge mounted at an angle in the wall.

Although the north (interior) sounding did not reach bedrock, it was dug to a depth of two meters. Some of the layers of fill contained Early Roman and earlier ceramic material, laid down during the Ayyūbid/Mamlūk period from earlier occupation accumulations in the vicinity. The south (exterior) sounding reached bedrock 2.61 m. below ground surface. All the layers of fill showed Ayyūbid/Mamlūk pottery. The lack of readable coins from most of the layers, plus the inability to distinguish and date the various types of pottery used during the two and a half centuries of these periods, made it impossible to determine the precise dates for the phases of the *Qasr* complex. But the sounding settled one thing—the south exterior of the Castle does not date from the Umayyad period as had occasionally been claimed.

*Cave G.4.*— On the basis of information from some villagers, Donald Wimmer and Timothy Smith inspected an extensive cave-cistern complex under the terrace west of the *Qasr*. Since the tomb excavation was nearing conclusion, they were assigned to make top plans, minor probes, and descriptive reports. From a large cave a partially filled passage led into a large, plastered cistern. This unplastered entryway was cut when the cisterns were used for human occupation, not water storage. Probes in the cistern produced Ayyūbid/Mamlūk and Byzantine sherds. Beyond the cistern was a central chamber from which three other cisterns had branched. The plastered complex may have been constructed in either Late or Early Roman times, but the early accumulations of silt layers had been removed to make the chambers habitable.

# THE TOPOGRAPHICAL SURVEY

S. DOUGLAS WATERHOUSE
Andrews University
Berrien Springs, Michigan

ROBERT IBACH, JR.
Grace Theological Seminary
Winona Lake, Indiana

## 1. Roman Road from Livias to Esbus (Fig. 10)

To trace the Roman road from Livias (modern *Tell er-Rameh*) in the Jordan Valley to Esbus (the Greek-Latin designation for Biblical Heshbon), a survey team of four was commissioned.[1] Long known but never completely traced, this Roman road connected Jerusalem, Jericho, Livias, and Esbus, thus linking the road system of Palestine with the famous north-south *via nova* of Trajan in the Roman province of Arabia, east of the Jordan (where Esbus/Heshbon is situated).[2]

Just as Trajan's north-south "new road" was built (A.D. 111-114) along the course of the much older Biblical "King's Highway" (Num 20:17; 21:22; cf. Gn 14:5, 6),[3] so the east-west road, from Jericho to Heshbon, was built near, if not always along, the Biblical "Way of Beth-Jeshimoth" (see the Hebrew text of Jos

[1] The survey team was to trace the Roman road from Esbus to the Jordan Valley and to obtain an archaeological picture of the occupational sites near *Tell Ḥesbân*, with special emphasis on the large valley, the *Wadi Ḥesbân*. Team members were S. Douglas Waterhouse, Robert Ibach, Charlene Hogsten, Eugenia Nitowski (part-time), and (as translators) the representatives of the Jordanian Department of Antiquities attached to the Heshbon Expedition.

[2] Peter Thomsen, "Die römischen Meilensteine der Provinzen Syria, Arabia und Palaestina," *ZDPV*, 40 (1917): 67-68; Michael Avi-Yonah, *The Holy Land* (Grand Rapids, Mich., 1966), pp. 183, 187 (map). For the most recent discussion of this road, see James Sauer, "Heshbon 1971: Area B," *AUSS*, 11 (1973): 54-56. The Roman province of Arabia with its highway *via nova* may have been established after the completion of the Livias-Esbus highway (see above in the text, and n. 3).

[3] Avi-Yonah, *Holy Land*, pp. 183, 187; Nelson Glueck: *AASOR*, 18-19 (1939): 143; see especially the comments of Sauer: "The north-south road, which became the *via nova*, could have been in existence before 111-114" ("Heshbon 1971," p. 56).

12:3). [4] It seems that the Romans did not establish new routes, but rather improved old roads.

It is not really known when the Romans laid down the Jericho-Livias-Esbus route as a highway for wheeled traffic,[5] possibly after the Jewish revolt of A.D. 66-73, when the Flavian emperors (A.D. 69-96) were consolidating their hold upon Palestine. If the tentative *Tell Ḥesbân* evidence—of roadway resurfacings (?) associated with a major stairway-gateway to the acropolis—proves meaningful, a Flavian date could be established.[6] It may have been done in preparation for the Emperor Hadrian's visit in A.D. 129, when considerable roadwork was done in this region.[7] Certainly the milestone inscriptions show that both the *via nova* and the Livias-Esbus road were repaired intermittently until the late fourth century.[8]

Since the southeastern flank of the Jordan Valley was a military zone, a survey party desiring freedom to roam the countryside could not start from that area, where three milestone stations of the road were already known. Instead, the team had to start from the *mishor*—the high tableland (Dt 3:10)—of ancient Moab, where *Tell Ḥesbân* is situated. From *Tell Ḥesbân,* access to the west is blocked by the deep valley of the *tell, Wadi el-Majjar.* Hence it was concluded that the ancient road from Esbus must first have gone southward, before turning westward, through the present-day village of *el-Mushaqqar,* on the westward fringe of the high *mishor*. This was confirmed by finding a single,

---

[4] Yohanan Aharoni, *The Land of the Bible: A Historical Geography* (Philadelphia, 1967), pp. 57, 40 (map). Note that the Roman road, unlike the OT "way," did not pass through Beth-jeshimoth. The name is reflected in modern *Khirbet Sweimeh,* though Glueck, followed by others, would identify the site with *Tell ʿAẓeimeh;* see his "Some Ancient Towns in the Plains of Moab," *BASOR,* No. 91 (Oct., 1943): 24-25, 14 (map).

[5] The Livias-Esbus road up the steep ascent from the Jordan Valley was evidently a well-built, graded highway intended for wheeled traffic.

[6] Sauer, "Heshbon, 1971," pp. 49-57.

[7] Avi-Yonah, *Holy Land,* pp. 183-184.

[8] Thomsen, *Meilensteine,* pp. 14, 35-57, 93. The Livias-Esbus road remained in use long after the fourth century; indeed Bedouins still use it today.

fragmented milestone—possibly the second mile from Esbus—
lying on its side (at grid reference 2248.1333), more than halfway
between *Tell Hesbân* and *el-Mushaqqar*.[9]

Then a villager at *el-Hawwaya*, a hamlet immediately west of
*el-Mushaqqar*, reported the existence, 20 to 30 years ago, of a
group of collapsed *serâbît* (the Bedouin expression for "milestone"). His report carried weight, for the eastern end of *el-Hawwaya* is exactly where the next milestone station (the third?)
would have been expected.

At the western edge of *el-Hawwaya* (grid reference 2225.1337),
where the westbound traveler first views the deep Jordan Valley,
a stone marker (?) was discovered, much smaller than a Roman
milestone but reminiscent of one. It had been cut by a professional, with a square shaft, but a base in the same rectangular
style as a milestone,[10] and it stood exactly where the Roman road
begins its dramatic descent toward the *Ghor*.[11]

From this vantage point the ridge, called like the village
*el-Mushaqqar* (Pl. XIII:A), slowly descends into the Jordan Valley. Affording a breath-taking view of the northern end of the
Dead Sea and the "plains of Moab" (Num 33:48), the Roman
road follows the crest of this ridge down to the ruin mound of the
city of Livias. The top of Mt. Nebo (*Jebel en-Nebā*) and the im-

---

[9] The milestone was first spotted on July 5 close to *'Ain Mūhrā*, which
marks the southernmost reaches of the *Wadi el-Majjar*, perched on the edge
of a ledge above the precipitous *wadi*. Five days later this unique marker was
found badly splintered. The local inhabitants had broken it open, believing
that the great interest shown in it by foreigners indicated treasure. A local
man told us that he believed the stone pointed toward hidden gold.

This badly-weathered milestone, about 2,500 m. southwest of *Tell Hesbân*
on the Roman road, is too far for the first milestone and too near for the
second, since a Roman mile is about 1,500 m. (one thousand "double paces"
or 1,479 m.). If the stone had been moved, it more likely represents mile two,
500 m. uphill to the west, than mile one, 1,000 m. mostly downhill to the east.

[10] Like the milestone at *'Ain Mūhrā* (cf. n. 9), this marker also was smashed
by villagers within a few days after discovery.

[11] It is at this very spot that the Roman road itself first becomes visible for
the modern westbound traveler. Since the marker in question was found at
the very edge of the ancient roadbed, it is difficult to dissociate this interesting
stone from the ancient highway.

posing promontory of Pisgah ( *Rās eṣ-Ṣiyāghah* )[12] form a parallel ridge, lying to the south of the *el-Mushaqqar* ridge, adding to the truly magnificent scenery. Between these two ridges is the *Wadi ʿAyūn Mūsā*, its springs making it a green valley in the midst of a desert landscape. The OT called this oasis "the valley opposite Beth-Peor" (Dt 3:29; 4:46; 34:6), or "the valley in the land of Moab near the top of Pisgah which rises up opposite Jeshimon" (Num 21:20),[13] probably the "slopes of Pisgah" (Jos 13:20; Dt 3:17; 4:49).[14] As will be seen, this information helps identify the route of the road.

At the base of the first precipitous descent of the ridge of *el-Mushaqqar* (grid reference 2217.1342), was another milestone station, presumably the fourth from Esbus,[15] where 24 milestone fragments, two of them with almost illegible inscriptions, lay strewn on the ground or half buried (Pl. XI:A). Obviously the stone fragments had been tumbled about by the repeated wash

---

[12] *En-Nebā*, the highest summit of the ridge, is assumed with good reason to be Biblical Mount Nebo. West-northwest of this summit there is a lower platform, *Ras eṣ-Ṣiyāghah*, which affords a larger and less obstructed panorama than that of the summit. The latter site, therefore, is thought to be the actual place of the Pisgah vision of Dt 34:1-3. The name *Ṣiyāghah*, found neither in the Bible nor in pilgrims' texts, originated from a Christian monastery built on the site (Aramaic: *Ṣiyāghah*, "the monastery"). See Sylvester J. Saller, *The Memorial of Moses on Mount Nebo* (3 vols.; Jerusalem, 1941-1950), 1: 116-117.

[13] "Jeshimon" *(KJV)*, which means "a waste, a desert," is taken to designate a specific desert, the region of Beth-Jeshimoth, northeast of the Dead Sea. *Jeshimon* can at times be a proper name: see 1 Sa 23:24, where "Jeshimon" is distinguished from "the desert *(midbār)* of Maon" to the south of it. See J. Simons, *The Geographical and Topographical Texts of the Old Testament* (Leiden, 1959), pp. 22-23. According to Num 21:29 Jeshimon is dominated, at least in part, by Pisgah; according to Num 23:28 by the top ("head") of the neighboring promontory to the north of Pisgah, Mount Peor.

[14] While A. H. Van Zyl would identify the Ashdoth-pisgah, "the slopes of Pisgah," with the *Wadi ʿAyūn Mūsa (The Moabites* [Leiden, 1960], p. 53), Simons would understand the designation as referring to the western slopes of *Ras eṣ-Ṣiyāghah* "which descends towards the Dead Sea basin and the 'fields of Moab' . . ." (*Texts of OT*, p. 65). Since Jos 13:20 lists "the slopes of Pisgah" as one of a number of towns and cities, we would tend to agree with the conclusions of Van Zyl. The *KJV* translates the phrase as the "springs of Pisgah" in Dt 4:49.

[15] Approximately 6,000 m. from *Tell Ḥesbân,* or about four Roman miles from ancient Esbus.

of the severe winter rains, which can cause severe local flooding. The 15 fragments with "square" bases indicated that the road had been repaired, or reconstructed, at least 15 times, for with each repair work a new milestone was erected, bearing the current emperor's name.

Approximately 1,500 m. further to the west (grid reference 2203.1341) is a place called *Serâbît el-Mushaqqar* where 13 fragments of 12 milestones lay scattered over a large area (Pl. XI:B).[16] Two of these venerable markers are still upright; four bear traces of inscriptions, two of which mention the fifth mile, probably from Esbus. These Latin inscriptions have been dated to the years 219, 307, and 364-375 (?).[17]

The sixth Roman mile station from Esbus, again about 1,500 m. from the fifth, was located at a dramatic promontory called *Khirbet el-Meḥaṭṭa*, a place of special significance. From information gathered from two fourth-century writers. Eusebius and the pilgrim Egeria (sometimes called Aetheria), it is learned that from this vantage point the traveler from Livias to Esbus could see Mt. Nebo and could, like Egeria, take a side path to 'Ayūn Mūsā and Mount Nebo.[18] They also inform us that at this promontory (*Meḥaṭṭa*) was the infamous Beth-Peor (Dt 4:46),[19]

[16] The site looks very much as it did to Saller in 1941 (*Memorial*, 1: 6-7; 2: Plate 6, 1).

[17] Thomsen, *Meilensteine*, p. 67.

[18] Eusebius, *Onomasticon*, with Jerome's Latin translation (ed. by Erich Klostermann [Hildesheim, 1966]), p. 16, lines 25-26, p. 18, line 1 (Jerome's trans., p. 17, lines 26-28); 136, 6-8 (137, 5-7); *Egeria's Travels*, chap. 10, sec. 8 (trans. by John Wilkinson [London, 1971]), p. 106. See the full discussion in Saller, *Memorial*, 1: 334, 335, and n. 2.

[19] Eusebius says that "Bethphogor," Biblical Bethpeor, was a city six miles from Livias near Mount Phogor, or Peor (*Onom.* 48, 3-5, [49, 3-4]), the mountain on which "Beelphegor" (Baal-peor) was worshiped (*Onom.* 44, 15-16 [45, 17-18]), and where Balak brought Balaam, overlooking Livias (*Onom.* 168, 25-26, [169, 19-20]), to curse Israel. Egeria records that from the church on Mount Nebo (*Siyāghah*) she could look north and see the city of "Fogor," or Peor (*Travels* 12. 8, p. 108). On Egeria (Aetheria), see Saller, *Memorial*, 1: 150, 151. On Beth-Peor see Oswald Henke, "Zur Lage von Beth Peor," *ZDPV*, 75 (1959): 155-163. Henke concludes that what Alois Musil (in *Arabia Petraea* [1907], 1: 344, 348) called "chirbet esch-schech dschājil" (*Khirbet esh-Sheik Jāyel*) is actually *Khirbet el-Meḥaṭṭa*.

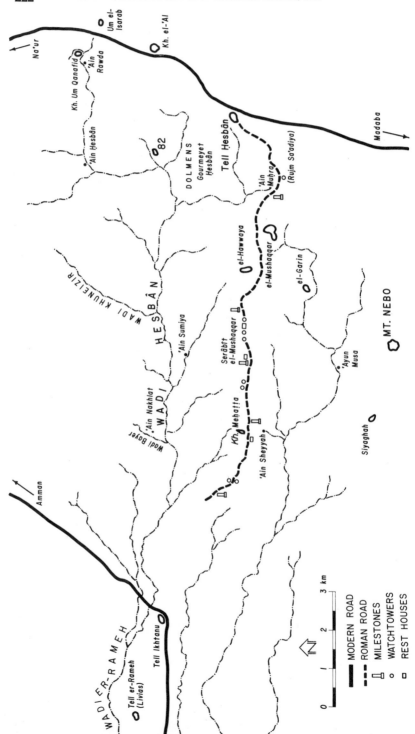

**Fig. 10.** Map of the area explored by the topographical survey team of the 1973 Heshbon expedition.

the high place of Baal from which Balaam saw the Israelite (Num 23:28) camp on the plains of Moab.[20]

This identification of the sixth milestone station with Beth-Peor (the "house of Phogor" in the *LXX* and classical sources) tallies with the OT information: Balaam (Num 31:16; cf. Rev 2:14) made the temple of Baal Peor a focal point for an "apostate" Israel (Num 25:1-3; Ps 106:28; Mic 6:5); thus the Hebrew encampment was near Mount Peor. Both neighboring mountain spurs, Pisgah and Beth-Peor, overlooked the same desert region of Jeshimon (Num 21:20; 23:28),[21] and Moses died and was buried in the region of Nebo/Pisgah (Dt 34:1, 5, 6) opposite Beth-Peor.[22] The ridge *el-Mushaqqar* with its western promontory, *Khirbet el-Meḥaṭṭa*, is the only ridge directly facing the burial place of Moses (the valley of *'Ayūn Mūsā*) and the slopes of *Rās eṣ-Ṣiyāghah*.

*Khirbet el-Meḥaṭṭa*, with its strategic view of the *Ghor*, now treeless and desolate under a burning sun, must have been once an oasis restful to both the eye and the body, with its flourishing grove of shade trees and its nearby spring, *'Ain Sheyyah*.[23] The ruined walls, gates and towers of a comparatively large Roman fortress (grid reference 2186.1341) are now all that remain of this important center (Fig. 11). Most of the sherds picked up at the site were Byzantine or Roman.

[20] Specifically, the *'Arbôth Mô'ab* was the southeastern Jordan Valley floor between the present-day *Wadi Nimrîn* (in the north) and the *Wadi el-'Azeimeh* (in the south, near the northeast end of the Dead Sea).

[21] See above, n. 13.

[22] In Deuteronomy, Moses apparently died in the locality of Nebo/Pisgah, but was buried in "the valley." That valley, elsewhere called the "Slopes of Pisgah" (see above, n. 14), obviously is *Wadi 'Ayūn Mūsa*. The Arabic name itself, "the springs of Moses" reflects a long-standing tradition relating this valley to Moses. See the discussion in Saller, *Memorial*, 1: 343, 344 and accompanying notes. Compare also Dt 3:29 and 4:46.

[23] Ancient pagan high places were noted for their groves of trees (Hos 4:13). In 1941 a tree still was to be seen standing at *el-Meḥaṭṭa;* see Saller, *Memorial*, 2: Plate 11, 1. The name *Sheyyah* refers to a type of desert scrub-brush which has completely overgrown the ancient spring (which used to be called *'Ain Meḥaṭṭa*).

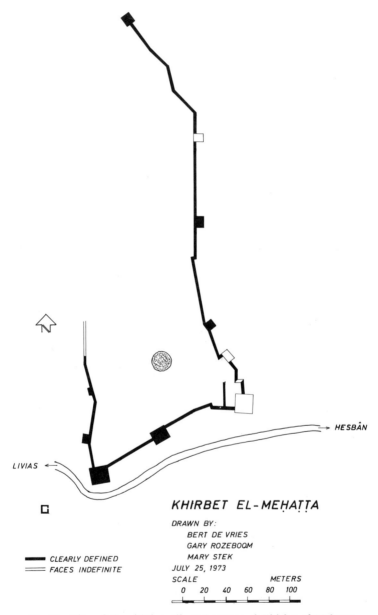

Fig. 11.  Plan of the visible walls and towers of *Khirbet el-Meḥaṭṭa*.

As the Roman road approaches (grid reference 2188.1340) the *Meḥaṭṭa* promontory, four milestones lie strewn over the ground. Today a single, barely visible inscription remains out of the three legible ones reported 30 to 60 years ago[24] mentioning the sixth mile from Esbus and dated 162, 235 and 288.[25]

West of the *Meḥaṭṭa* promontory, the grade of the road is quite steep down to the valley floor. Consequently the five extant milestones presumably marking the seventh mile from Esbus have washed downhill and now rest 2,100 m. from the sixth mile station (grid reference 2170.1348). They could not have tumbled too great a distance, for they lie either on the ancient roadbed or immediately nearby; and they are not far from a possible rest station (grid reference 2172.1344/1345), a place usually associated with the erection of mile markers.[26] These milestones must have marked the seventh mile from Esbus, yet we cannot satisfactorily account for their tumbling down the winding road for the remarkable distance of some 650 m.![27]

These five separate milestone stations, marking the second (?), fourth, fifth, sixth, and seventh (?) Roman miles from Esbus, of course establish definitely the route of the Roman road. Almost nowhere except on the *el-Mushaqqar* ridge is the worn bed of what once had been an intensively traveled highway still visible. Here and there, marking the edges, are rows of tightly fitted curbstones and occasionally the remains of small, worn, irregular cobblestones (Pl. XII:A).[28] The width of the road averaged about

[24] Thomsen, *Meilensteine*, pp. 67-68, Nos. 229-231; Saller, *Memorial*, 1: 334, n. 2.

[25] Thomsen, *Meilensteine*, pp. 67-68. Note the remarks of Eusebius in n. 19.

[26] The so-called "rest station" actually consists of the ruined foundations of two circular towers. However, the plateau site would have been a natural rest area for travelers. Rest houses need not always have been situated at a given mile station. See n. 32.

[27] Compare above, n. 9, noting that a single milestone seems to have been moved some 500 m. from its original position.

[28] In places where the Roman road was comparably well preserved, not only were curbstones preserved on either side of the highway, but also a center string of tightly-fitted stones remains—evidence that the surface for the road had been raised in the center, sloping on both sides. This was a characteristic

six meters.[29] The first curb stones appeared just beyond the Roman marker (?) at *el-Hawwaya* (grid reference 2222.1339), the last at the point where the road began to level off for "long dropping runs" down into the Jordan Valley (grid reference 2167.1352).

The foundation-remains of rest/way houses and watchtowers along the way were spotted frequently, sherded, and measured. Along the entire *el-Mushaqqar* ridge were found the remains— at times almost mere rubble—of seven circular watchtowers (or guard posts?), spaced irregularly along the crest of the ridge (grid references 2214.1341, 2211.1342, 2209.1342, 2198.1342, 2197.1342, 2172.1344, 2172.1345).[30] Their deterioration in modern times is evidenced by a picture of one of them in a 1941 publication showing a second course of stone blocks.[31] Dating was difficult because of the paucity and the simple character of the ceramic fragments, and their erosion from the hilltop sites. Yet the predominance of pottery from Byzantine and Roman times, the era of the Roman road, was established (Pl. XIII:B).

A pile of rubble-stones (locally named *Rujm Sa'adiya*), west of the second (?) milestone marker may be the remains of a resthouse, though more likely of a watchtower (grid reference 2250.1332). Rectangular foundations of probable resthouses were discovered near the fourth, fifth, and sixth milestone stations.[32]

feature of Trajan's *via nova*. Compare the recent remarks of Z. Kallai, "Remains of the Roman Road Along the Mevo-Beitar Highway," *IEJ*, 15 (1965): 203.

[29] The widths measured from 4.90 to 11.20 m.

[30] The diameters of these seven towers ranged from 5.90 m. to 9.30 m. The tower foundations usually consisted of three rows of stone blocks. That these towers were actually defensive lookout stations is suggested by the fact that they were found not only in connection with the Roman road; remains of identical structures were spotted also in the ridges to the north.

[31] Saller, *Memorial*, 2: Plate 11, 2.

[32] One, at the fifth station, had been rebuilt in comparatively modern times, but only its four walls still stand. Immediately east of this rebuilt rest station (3.90 x 6.65 m.) was the foundation of an older structure, 4.35 x 5.25 m. No traces of any structure were found at the site marking the fourth mile from Esbus, but about 375 m. to the east were well-preserved foundations of what presumably was a resthouse (4.50 x 4.70 m.). The four milestones marking

The city of Livias, identified by classical sources with Beth-haram (Num 32:36; Jos 13:27), is on linguistic grounds associated with the modern name *Tell er-Rameh* (Beth-haram became *Beth-ramtha, Beit er Ram,* and then *Tell er-Rameh*).[33] In recent decades however, this identification with modern *Tell er-Rameh* has been questioned because repeated sherding on the mound failed to produce any ceramic fragments dating before the Roman era.[34] This season, however, the Heshbon survey team did turn up evidence of earlier occupation back to the Iron I period (12th-11th centuries B.C.).[35] While this new ceramic evidence helps fix the traditional identification of *Tell er-Rameh*, there remains another argument in its favor: Eusebius' statement that Beth-Peor was situated by Mt. Phogor (Peor) opposite Jericho, six miles above Livias on the way to Esbus.[36] Since *Khirbet el-Meḥaṭṭa*/Beth-Peor is indeed approximately six Roman miles from *Tell er-Rameh*, it is hard to escape the conclusion that this latter *tell* (grid reference 2111.1371) contains the remains of ancient Livias.

Livias must have been especially significant to the eastbound traveler, being both the twelfth mile station from Esbus and the

the sixth mile from Esbus were about 300 m. east of the ruins—the *khirbet*—of the "Roman" fortress and related structures at *el-Meḥaṭṭa*.

[33] Glueck, "Ancient Towns," pp. 20-21; Simons, *Texts of OT*, p. 122.

[34] Glueck, "Ancient Towns," p. 21; *AASOR*, 25-28 (1951): 389-391. Following the convictions of W. F. Albright (*AASOR*, 6 [1924-1925]: 49) and Glueck, most scholars have identified *Tell Ikhtanū* as the site of ancient Beth-haram/Livias. That *tell* has yielded pottery from the Iron Age, and it is a commanding site not too far from *Tell er-Rameh*. *Ikhtanū*, a large isolated hill, is about 2¾ km. east-southeast of *Tell er-Rameh*. It is situated about a half km. south of the *Wadi er-Rameh* (as the lower course of the *Wadi Ḥesbân* is known; see grid reference 2137.1364). A brief notice indicates that Kay Wright has excavated a Middle Bronze I settlement there (Paul W. Lapp, *Biblical Archaeology and History* [New York, 1969], p. 73 and Plate 13). The Heshbon survey team also sherded the mound, finding Byzantine, Roman, and Hellenistic periods represented, as well as the Iron Age; one possible Late Bronze sherd was also found. There is thus no doubt that *Tell Ikhtanū* presents a good candidate for Livias.

[35] Periods represented were: possible modern, Ottoman, Ayyūbid/Mamlūk, possible 'Abbāsid, Umayyad, Byzantine, Roman body sherds, Early Roman, Hellenistic, Iron II/Persian, Iron II, Iron I, and some unidentified sherds.

[36] See above, n.19.

spot where the land begins its first imperceptible rise from the center of the Jordan Valley;[37] and likewise another turning-point, a midway marker between Livias and Esbus—the lofty promontory of the house of Phogor/Peor. It is no wonder that classical sources, when speaking of this east-west highway, laid emphasis upon only three sites: Livias, Phogor, and Esbus.[38]

## 2. The Wadi Hesbân (Fig. 10)

Approximately 4¼ km. north northeast of Tell Hesbân lie the easternmost reaches of the Wadi Hesbân, which slopes down to the spring, 'Ain Rawda (grid reference 2282.1385), formerly called 'Ain Umm Qanafid. This important spring marks the start of what we may term the "Upper Wadi Hesbân," which extends some 3 km. west to the region of 'Ain Hesbân (grid reference 2256.1384). This narrow section of the wadi-bed, where at times the flanking hills tower steeply like confining walls, lacks running water during the four summer months.[39] Along the valley floor a number of rock-cut tombs of the single loculus type are found in the Roman style of construction.[40]

"Middle Wadi Hesbân" is the designation of the sayl, or "brook" Hesbân. In contrast to the Upper Wadi Hesbân, it is a wide garden-farm valley, watered by the springs of 'Ain Hesbân. From these springs the sayl Hesbân runs southward about 2 km., then in a wide swing westward for another 4¾ km. before narrowing in its dramatic plunge down toward the Jordan Valley. Here and there along the river bank are the ruins of ten ancient water wheels. Surface sherds in their vicinity may date them back to the

---

[37] Compare the remarks of Glueck, "Ancient Towns," p. 22. That Livias was a twelfth mile station from Esbus is assumed from the remarks of Eusebius (above, n. 19).

[38] See above, nn. 18, 19; also Saller, Memorial, 1: 334-335 (n. 2).

[39] This description excludes the perennial spring waters of 'Ain Rawda and the two major springs in the vicinity of 'Ain Hesbân. The Upper Wadi Hesbân cannot be described in desert terms. Oleanders, vineyards on the steep hills, and fig and pomegranate trees make the valley a green oasis.

[40] These grave shafts were not cut into the hillside, but rather were cut into large boulders that lie above the eroded channel of the wadi.

Ayyūbid/Mamlūk period, though this remains speculative.[41]

In the region of the hillside oasis of 'Ain Sumiya (grid reference 2230.1362), the wide valley changes to the narrow, sharply descending "Lower Wadi Ḥesbân," running almost directly westward in a deep gorge, then breaking out from the high tableland and flowing into the wide Jordan Valley near Tell Ikhtanū (grid reference 2137.1364). Here, some 7 km. west of 'Ain Sumiya, it becomes known as the Wadi er Rameh.

Surface sherding indicates, in much of the valley, Ottoman, Ayyūbid/Mamlūk, Byzantine, Roman, and Iron II/Persian occupation. The Umayyad period is but weakly represented, except in spots along the eastern flank of the Middle Wadi Ḥesbân; the Hellenistic period only at the headwaters of the Upper Wadi Ḥesbân and from the region of 'Ain Sumiya downward into the valley floor of the Lower Wadi Ḥesbân; Iron I nowhere except at the Upper Wadi Ḥesbân, where at times it is the dominant ware.[42]

Searching through the valley floor of the Middle Wadi Ḥesbân, the survey team found small areas rather thickly strewn with Early Bronze pottery: small body sherds, tentatively dated, in the Bāla gardens (grid reference 2251.1375) near 'Ain Ḥesbân, but substantial fragments in the southwest end of the valley (especially grid references 2251.1362, 2238.1367, and 2235.1367).[43]

On the steep sides of Gourmeyet Ḥesbân (a large mountain mass lying between Tell Ḥesbân and the Middle Wadi Ḥesbân), are the remnants of an extensive dolmen field (grid references 2258.1352, 2250.1355, and 2252.1357)—ten dolmens, half of them still standing or partially standing. Though they look like houses, these large megalithic structures are thought to have served as

[41] One of these water wheels near 'Ain Ḥesbân is still in operation. No pottery remains dating to Ottoman times were found near these structures, but Ayyūbid/Mamlūk ware was abundant.

[42] The Lower Wadi Ḥesbân was not explored west of the Wadi Bayer region (grid reference 2182.1362) near 'Ain Nakhlat.

[43] The survey team found the same type of Early Bronze ware at Na'ur, again along the valley floor and the gentle hill slopes.

tombs. As elsewhere in the country, these monuments averaged about six feet high and upwards of twelve feet long. Their stones are of such stupendous size that neither earthquake, violent weather, nor time have had any serious effect in demolishing these structures (Pl. XII:B).

Though most scholars have dated their construction to the Pre-pottery Neolithic Age,[44] a 1966 sounding at *Shamir*, in northern Galilee, produced evidence that these megalithic structures date from the end of the Early Bronze Age or the beginning of the Middle Bronze I period.[45] Thus it is striking that from the whole of the Bronze Age, it is only from this period—beginning at the end of the third millennium, when newcomers invaded the country[46]—that *Gourmeyet Ḥesbân* has yielded quantities of sherds, many with the envelope ledge handles typical of the end of the Early Bronze Age.[47] In the light of this, and of the work done at *Shamir*, the question of whether these megalithic structures on *Gourmeyet Ḥesbân* date from the time of the envelope ledge handles seems pertinent.

Evidences of this late phase of the Early Bronze Age were found also on the other high, remote elevation-points that flank the Mid-

[44] See Emmanuel Anati, *Palestine Before the Hebrews* (New York, 1963), pp. 278-283; W. F. Albright, *The Archaeology of Palestine* (5th ed.; Baltimore, 1960), pp. 63-64; James L. Swauger, "Dolmen Studies in Palestine," *BA*, 24 (1966): 106-114.

[45] "The centre of the dolmen field apparently was occupied by a camp or temporary settlement, whose inhabitants built the dolmens." D. Bahat, "The Date of the Dolmens near Kibbutz Shamir," *IEJ*, 22 (1972): 44-46. See also the communication by Claire Epstein in "Notes and News," *IEJ*, 23 (1973): 109-110. Artifacts and a "wealth of pottery" excavated from dolmen fields in the Golan, during the summers of 1971 and 1972, indicated a construction date of ca. 2300-1950 B.C.

[46] That these newcomers, the so-called Amorites, "originated from a Mesopotamian sphere of influence rather than . . . the Caucasus or beyond . . .," is held, on the recent evidence, by Y. Yadin, "A Note on the Scenes Depicted on the 'Ain-Samiya Cup," *IEJ*, 21 (1971): 85 and n. 12.

[47] ". . . the folded jar handles are typologically intermediate between the typical pushed-up wavy ledge handles of E.B. III and the envelope handles which dominated the earlier part of the I-H complex at Tell Beit Mirsim." Albright, "The Chronology of Middle Bronze I (Early Bronze-Middle Bronze)," *BASOR*, No. 168 (Dec., 1962): 38.

dle *Wadi Ḥesbân*. The few Early Bronze body sherds collected from the valley floor of both Middle and Lower *Wadi Ḥesbân* probably represent sherds washed down from the heights. If so, these ceramic fragments would date to the time of the envelope ledge handles.

As for the other historical periods discovered at *Wadi Ḥesbân*, it is necessary to speak of three important ancient sites. The first is *Umm el-Îsarab* ("Ummīsareb" in the local dialect), a low hill commanding the eastern approach to the *wadi* (grid reference 2292.1379).[48] The name means "mother of trails," designating it as a center for converging paths. For here the ground begins to decline in a gradual, but steady, descent to the only major spring in the vicinity, *'Ain Rawda,* the source of the *Wadi Ḥesbân*. Surface finds indicated that *Umm el-Îsarab* thrived during Byzantine, [49] Roman, Hellenistic, and Iron I times. More significant for Transjordan's history are the sherds picked up here that are probably pre-Iron I, but not as early as the Early Bronze Age. Tentatively read as possible Middle/Late Bronze Age, they represent a rare type, seemingly endemic only to the tableland of Transjordan. This type of pottery has so far turned up only in burial caves and, unfortunately, not in controlled, stratified, archaeological contexts.[50]

The second site is *Khirbet Umm Qanafid* (grid reference 2284.1386), an independent hill within the *wadi*-bed itself, immediately east of the spring of *'Ain Rawda*. This fortress-like ancient city[51] is three-quarters surrounded by the moat-like, deep *wadi*-bed; its water made sure by the spring at its base. The sherds picked up from the *khirbet* yield a history somewhat

[48] *Umm el-Îsarab* is about 1½ km. north of *Khirbet el-'Al* (Biblical Elealeh) on the *Madeba-Na'ur* highway.

[49] Byzantine is the dominant ware to be found on the mound.

[50] Oral information from James A. Sauer.

[51] Villagers pointed out the remains of what they believed to be an ancient wall that encircles the *khirbet*. They also spoke of a tunnel near *'Ain Rawda*. From the top of the hill a jar handle of the Iron II/Persian period was obtained, inscribed with a large letter *beth*.

similar to that of *Tell Ḥesbân*: Modern,[52] Ottoman, Ayyūbid/
Mamlūk, Byzantine, Late and Early Roman, Hellenistic, Iron II/
Persian, and Iron I. One possible Middle Bronze (Hyksos
period) sherd and several possible Late Bronze sherds were
found in the *wadi*-bed directly below the *khirbet's* eastern flank.
These, together with the possible Middle Bronze Age samples
picked up by the survey team at two other places in Jordan's
high tableland, should alert the student to the danger of stating
that there was little or no occupation in Transjordan in the
Middle and Late Bronze Ages.[53]

Directly to the north of *Gourmeyet Ḥesbân* is a third important
site termed #82, the top plateau of a hill (grid reference
2258.1365) overlooking the Middle *Wadi Ḥesbân* at the curve
toward the west. The ceramic evidence from Site #82 ranged
from the Ottoman, Ayyūbid/Mamlūk, Byzantine, Roman, to
the Iron II/Persian period, with a major hiatus thence to Middle
Bronze I (two pieces of "caliciform" ware); then, by far the most
prevalent ware represented, the various Early Bronze phases,
especially III and IV.[54] Architectural remains attest this long

[52] The modern village of *Rawda* now encompasses the ancient site.

[53] Long ago Glueck deduced a gap in sedentary occupation of the Transjordan region from the 20th to the 13th centuries B.C. In recent years a number of scholars have raised questions concerning that thesis. See, for example,
the remarks of G. Lankester Harding, *The Antiquities of Jordan* (London,
1960), p. 33; Kathleen M. Kenyon, *Amorites and Canaanites* (London, 1966),
p. 64; H. J. Franken and W. J. A. Power, "Glueck's *Explorations in Eastern
Palestine* in the Light of Recent Evidence," *VT*, 21 (1971): 120-123. The survey team spent seven weeks examining archaeological remains within a ten-
kilometer radius of *Tell Ḥesbân*, as well as three tells in the Jordan Valley.
Ceramic ware possibly dating from the Middle Bronze Age (Hyksos period)
was found at *Tell Jalul* (grid reference 2312.1254) and in the region of *Na'ur*
(grid reference 2289.1424).

[54] On the northern flank of the *Wadi 'Ayūn Mūsa*, at a place called *el-Garin*
(grid reference 2223.1324), the survey team discovered a once heavily settled
Early Bronze site. Both Site 82 and *el-Garin* represent Early Bronze Age
settlements nestled in large *wadi*-valleys that run down from the high tableland to the Jordan Valley; nowhere else did the survey team find Early
Bronze Age sherds in such quantities. In this connection it is of interest that
in the course of this survey, Early Bronze Age sherds were found on the
western slope of *Tell Ḥesbân* (grid reference 2263.1343).

span of human occupation.[55]

In conclusion, on the basis of the pottery[56] found in this surface examination of much of the *Wadi Ḥesbân* a varied and checkered archaeological history emerges, from the modern period to the Early Bronze Age. Future excavation of selected sites in the *Wadi Ḥesbân* could serve to check and to fill out this tentative history.

[55] The discovery of Site 82 may be especially significant for the ongoing discussion on the late Early Bronze-Middle Bronze I cultural complex. For Site 82, with what may amount to an unbroken cultural sequence, from "Early Bronze III" to "Middle Bronze I," would thus be an exception to the majority of cities, which were devastated during the Early Bronze II-III periods and then abandoned. Soundings and a closer analysis of the materials at 82 could possibly reveal this as a site showing a clear sequence from the "Early Bronze IV" forms down to the elements of classic "Middle Bronze I." As of yet, "nowhere is there a single site which spans the entire period"; so in William G. Dever, "The **EB IV-MB I** Horizon in Transjordan and Southern Palestine," *BASOR*, No. 210 (Apr., 1973): 41, and cf. pp. 56-57; see also his "The 'Middle Bronze I' Period in Syria and Palestine," *Near Eastern Archaeology in the Twentieth Century,* ed. James A. Sanders (New York, 1970), p. 150 and n. 87.

[56] The sherds collected during the survey were washed and read in camp and a representative number were saved and registered for future reference. Those not registered were discarded on the dump of potsherds at *Tell Ḥesbân.*

# THE ANTHROPOLOGICAL WORK

ØYSTEIN AND ASTA SAKALA LABIANCA
Boston, Massachusetts

This preliminary report briefly describes the anthropological work carried out by the authors and their assistants during the 1973 season of excavations at Tell Ḥesbân.[1] It also attempts to interpret a portion of the data collected. The first section of the report will discuss activities such as 1) bone reading, 2) assembling of a comparative collection, 3) conducting a topographical bone survey, and 4) carrying out ethnographical studies. It will also describe the method used for describing, recording, and analyzing the animal bones recovered. The second section will deal with some of the findings, discuss some of the problems encountered, and explain some of the methods used in solving the problems.

## Supportive Activities

In order to provide the Area and Square supervisors with a regular preliminary report on the number and species identification of bones recovered from each locus, a weekly "bone reading" was carried out at the field station. These sessions provided the archaeologists with up-to-date information on the animal remains recovered, and the anthropologists with information about the archaeological context from which the bones came.

[1] The following individuals deserve a special word of gratitude for their willingness to lend a helping hand during the last few days of the expedition, when "scribes" were at a premium, to get the data recorded: Eugenia Nitowski, Nahla R. Abbouski, Tom Meyer, Avery Dick, and Rick Mannell. Mohammad Saied's helpfulness as a translator and informant was also much appreciated. The first-named author also wants to thank the Zion Research Foundation, Boston, Massachusetts, for a travel scholarship which enabled him to participate in the expedition.

An important achievement of last summer's expedition was the assembling of possibly the first osteological comparative collection in Jordan. It consists of unbroken skeletal remains of sheep, goat, cattle, donkey, horse, camel, dog, cat, and chicken. These, collected by the authors in the fields surrounding the modern village of Ḥesbân, facilitated greater accuracy in identifying the more than 7,000 bone fragments of domestic species[2] found during the excavations.

A topographical bone survey was conducted in conjunction with assembling the comparative collection. This consisted of a random crisscrossing of the fields surrounding Ḥesbân and the grounds inside the village. The survey aided us in observing patterns related to the deposition of animal remains. An especially interesting finding relates to the remains of food animals versus non-food animals; *all* the bones of the donkey, horse, dog, or cat skeletons were found, whereas bones of sheep, goat, and cattle were mostly from meat-poor sections like skulls or extremities. An exception would be sheep or goats killed by predators. In such cases, the skin of the animals and large portions of their skeletons were found.

Ethnographic inquiries were initiated with the specific goal of compiling data that would shed light on the problems arising from the analysis of the animal remains. The butchering and consumption of two sheep and two goat carcasses at a *mensef* feast were witnessed by one of the authors. In particular, observations were made of meat-cutting and carcass-utilization practices. Husbandry practices such as those related to herd management and herd composition were also noted.

Fourteen categories of information were delineated for describing each bone fragment.[3] Categories 4, 5, and 7-13 were used only where applicable.

[2] Macerated and sun-bleached bones were plentiful in the fields surrounding the village.

[3] We developed a "recording guide" to enable us to write in the data with maximum efficiency and at the same time make subsequent sorting easier.

1. Find spot—the Area letter, and the Square, pail and locus numbers for the place in which the bone fragment was found.

2. Taxonomy—the kind of animal the bone represented (e.g., sheep, or goat, cattle, etc.).

3. Element—the name of the bone as it related to the complete skeleton (e.g., humerus, radius, etc.).

4. Fusion—the state of the epiphysial union in the bone: whether fused, partially fused, or unfused.

5. Element modifier—if the bone was an element with sub-categories (e.g., phalanges can be first, second, or third), the sub-category.

6. Fragment description—a description of each bone fragment, using a letter for its fragment type, and a number for its approximate size, "measured" on a scale of concentric circles numbered from 1 to 25 and with radii increasing by 10 mm. to 250 mm. (e.g., B7 indicates a "B" type of fragment on a bone of 70 mm. size).

7. Thermal effects—any signs of a bone having been cooked or roasted, and the color of the burn mark.

8. Right or left—whether the bone was from the right or left side of the animal.

9. Special—a notation of pathology or other irregularities not covered by any of the other categories.

10. Sex—pelvic features most often pertinent.

11. Cultural marks—any signs of cutting, chopping, piercing, etc., the location of these marks on the bone being pinpointed by comparison with a model drawing of the element prepared with a lettered horizontal scale and a numbered vertical scale.

12. Physical condition—whether the bone was in poor physical condition; i.e., if it was crumbling, had a pitted surface, etc.

13. Animal marks—any rodent chews, dog bites, etc. on the bone.

14. Measurements, where desired—length, width, height, and circumference of such parts as metapodial condyles.

Currently we are engaged in the analysis and interpretation of the 1973 materials. We are developing a computer program which will enable us to handle large retrieval jobs such as are

It consisted of a card with 17 rectangular 10 x 30 mm. openings cut out, one each for 13 of the above information categories, and four for the 14th, to accommodate all possible measurements made on one bone. This instrument enabled us to record all the necessary information for each bone on a standard data card 6 cm. x 14 cm. We found that this method, using the 14 information categories and a recording guide, has almost unlimited flexibility and convenience for sorting. It has been easily adapted to computerization by transforming the 14 information categories into "fields" contained on a standard 80-column data card. Key-punching was simplified by having the data cards sorted by element and then by species. Thus best possible use could be made of auto-duplication in the key-punch process.

required in analyzing zooarchaeological data.[4]

## Preliminary Results

By utilizing ethnographic observations of the butchering and carcass utilization practices of the present-day villagers of Ḥesbân it has been possible to make inferences about some of the practices of the inhabitants of the *tell* in the Late Roman and Hellenistic periods.

Our study is based on an analysis of remains of sheep and goat from two Hellenistic loci, D.1:59 and D.1:60, and from two Late Roman loci, D.2:36 and D.2:40. The samples from these loci were selected because they had the largest number of bones from clear contexts available at the time of writing this report.

In antiquity, sheep and goats were the most popular food animals during all periods of occupation at *Tell Ḥesbân,*[5] just as they are today in modern Ḥesbân. In contrast to the present-day villagers, whose herds are composed of only slightly more sheep than goats, the ancient villagers seem to have had a generally stronger preference for sheep. Of the bones for which separation was possible (a few well preserved long bones, scapulae, and pelves), 17 came from sheep and two from goats in the Hellenistic loci; seven came from sheep and two from goats in the Late Roman loci.

Today's villagers maintain mixed herds composed mostly of mature females of each species, with usually only one or two mature males in each flock. Males are presumably slaughtered while still young. Even though there were few bones in our samples, they do indicate that females outnumbered males. For the bones for which separation was possible, two were females and one was male in the Hellenistic sample, and one was female in the Late Roman sample.

---

[4] John Lindquist and Paul Perkins, both computer programmers, have been assisting with this project.

[5] Øystein LaBianca, "The Zooarchaeological Remains from *Tell Ḥesbân,*" *AUSS,* 11 (1973): 133-144.

The age at which an animal is slaughtered can be estimated from postcranial remains by studying rates of fusion of the epiphysis.[6] Table 1 shows counts (grouped as in Hole and Flannery) of fused versus unfused epiphyses among sheep and goats from the four loci. By adding the number of fused bones in each group within a sample and then computing the percentage of the total number of fused and unfused bones in the same group that this sum represents, it is possible to obtain a percentage estimate of the survival rates of sheep and goats of various ages. Because the samples had so few bones, the Hellenistic samples and the Late Roman samples were combined, respectively; and groups A and B and groups C and D (see Table 1) were combined, respectively, as follows:

| GROUP | BONE | D.1: 59  HEL. | | D.1: 60  HEL. | | D.2: 36  L.R. | | D.2: 40  L.R. | |
|---|---|---|---|---|---|---|---|---|---|
| | | F | U | F | U | F | U | F | U |
| A. FUSING WITHIN ONE YEAR | RADIUS PR | 3 | | 2 | | 1 | | 1 | |
| | HUMERUS DI | 2 | 1 | 1 | | | 2 | | |
| | SCAPULA | 1 | 1 | | | | | | |
| | PELVIS | | | 1 | | 2 | 1 | 3 | |
| B. 2 YEARS | TIBIA DI | 2 | 1 | 1 | 1 | 1 | | 2 | 1 |
| C. 2.5 YEARS | METAPOD DI | 3 | 1 | 2 | | 4 | 1 | 2 | 2 |
| D. 3- 3.5 YEARS | FEMUR PR | 2 | 2 | | 2 | 1 | 2 | | |
| | FEMUR DI | | | | | | | | 1 |
| | RADIUS DI | 1 | | | 1 | | 1 | | |
| | TIBIA PR | 1 | | | | | | | |

Table 1. Raw counts of fused versus unfused epiphyses among sheep and goats from four loci.

For the Hellenistic samples, 76% of the bones from groups A and B and 60% from groups C and D were fused. For the Late Roman sample, 71% of the bones from groups A and B and 50% from groups C and D were fused. These findings suggest that sheep and goats had a relatively shorter life expectancy during the Late Roman period than during the Hellenistic period.

[6] Frank Hole, Kent V. Flannery, and James A. Neeley, *Prehistory and Human Ecology of the Deh Luran Plain*, Memoirs of the Museum of Anthropology, University of Michigan, no. 1 (Ann Arbor, 1969).

Table 2 shows measurements (in centimeters) of the width (w) of the distal end of the metacarpals and metatarsals, and the diameter of the outer condyle (n) and the inner condyle (m) of the distal epiphysis of the metapodials for the four samples. The largest number of measurements was possible from metapodials in the Late Roman sample from D.2:36. A comparison of the measurements reveals that as a group the measurements of bones from the Late Roman samples are slightly larger than those from the Hellenistic samples.

| BONE | D.1: 59 HEL. | | | D.1: 60 HEL. | | | D.2: 36 L.R. | | | D.2: 40 L.R. | | |
|---|---|---|---|---|---|---|---|---|---|---|---|---|
| | W | N | M | W | N | M | W | N | M | W | N | M |
| METACARPAL | 2.68 | 1.61 | 0.91 | | 1.61 | 0.91 | | 1.81 | 1.31 | | | |
| | | | | | | | | 2.17 | 1.26 | | | |
| | | | | | | | | 1.73 | 1.19 | | | |
| METATARSAL | | 1.73 | 1.18 | | | | 2.57 | 1.69 | 1.05 | 2.77 | 1.71 | 1.16 |
| | | | | | | | 3.02 | 1.85 | 1.25 | | | |

Table 2. Measurements (in centimeters) of the distal ends of nine metapodials of sheep and goats from four loci.

Table 3 illustrates the average size of the fragments of the respective elements recovered, based on the data obtained by measuring each fragment. The sample from D.1:59 shows that bones of the forelimb (scapula, humerus, and radius) were represented by larger fragments than bones of the hind limb (femur and tibia). In the Late Roman samples (from D.2:36 and D.2:40) metacarpals were represented by larger fragments than were the metatarsals. In a Late Roman sample from D.2:36 the mean size of fragments was larger (4.1 cm.) than in the other three samples (approximately 3.1 cm. for each).

The fact that the majority of the skeletal remains recovered were incomplete fragments, such as distal or proximal ends or shafts of long bones, leads one to ask the question: Who or what fragmented these bones, and how?

The possibility that some bones may have been fragmented simply by being trodden upon by man and beast has been suggested by findings from a study that compared the condition of the bones from an enclosed cistern environment with bones from a regular layer.[7]

| BONE | D.I: 59 HEL. | D.I: 60 HEL. | D.2: 36 L.R. | D.2: 40 L.R. |
|------|--------------|--------------|--------------|--------------|
| SCAPULA | 43/11  3.91 | 6/2  3.00 | 2/1  2.00 | |
| HUMERUS | 11/13  3.66 | 12/4  3.00 | 10/3  3.33 | |
| RADIUS | 24/16  4.00 | | 37/10  3.70 | 2/1  2.00 |
| ULNA | | | 3/1  3.00 | |
| PELVIS | 2/1  2.00 | 16/5  3.20 | 20/6  3.33 | 13/5  2.60 |
| FEMUR | 8/3  2.66 | | 12/2  6.00 | 3/1  3.00 |
| TIBIA | 14/5  2.80 | 9/3  3.00 | 3/1  3.00 | 37/10  3.70 |
| METACARPAL | 21/6  3.50 | 9/3  3.00 | 53/12  4.41 | 39/9  4.33 |
| METATARSAL | 10/4  2.50 | 13/3  4.33 | 18/5  3.60 | 37/10  3.70 |
| CENTIMETERS: | 1  2  3  4  5 | 1  2  3  4  5 | 1  2  3  4  5 | 1  2  3  4  5 |

Table 3. Average size of fragments of some elements of sheep and goats from four loci. In the fraction above each bar, the numerator is the sum of the individual fragment measurements; the denominator is the number of fragments measured.

It is likely, however, judging from cut marks observed on bone fragments, that many bones were fragmented as a result of butchering and meat cutting. This explanation is supported by observations of present-day practices.

The villagers of modern Ḥesbân slaughter their sheep and goats on the grounds outside their dwellings. Holding the front two legs of the animal in his left hand and pressing the neck to the ground with his right foot, the villager slits the animal's throat with a knife. After the blood has drained for a few minutes he completely severs the head between the occipital bone and the atlas.

In preparation for the skinning, the forefeet are amputated

[7] Øystein LaBianca: "A Study of Postcranial Remains of Sheep and Goat from *Tell Ḥesbân*, Jordan" (unpublished manuscript, Harvard University, Spring, 1973), pp. 53, 54.

between the distal end of the radius and the proximal end of the metacarpal bone to facilitate the removal of the skin. Then an incision is made at the distal end of the left tibia separating the bone and the flesh so that a rope can be threaded through and the carcass hoisted up the side wall of one of the dwellings. While thus suspended by one hind leg the carcass is skinned and the internal organs removed. The remaining carcass is sectioned as follows: the two forelimbs are separated by dissecting the scapula away from the trunk; the left half of the rib cage is partially separated by cuts—starting at the caudal end— severing the proximal end of the rib from the rest of it; the sternum is cut away from the partially separated left half of the rib cage; the neck, including the atlas, axis, and 4th-5th cervical vertebrae, is sectioned off; the fat tail is cut off at the caudal end of the sacrum; the right half of the rib cage is separated; the vertebral column is divided into two sections, one consisting of approximately three cervical vertebrae and six thoracic vertebrae, the other of the seven remaining thoracic vertebrae and two lumbar vertebrae; the right hind foot is cut off between the proximal end of the metatarsal and the distal end of the tibia and discarded; the right hind limb is removed by severing the muscles and sinews binding it to the pelvis; finally, the left hind limb is loosened from the rope and the left hind foot is cut off in the same manner as the right hind foot, and discarded.

The major post-cranial sections seen in this butchering practice are: two forelimbs, two forefeet, two halves of the rib cage, the sternum, five vertebral column sections, two hind limbs, and two hind feet. For the most part, the bones themselves were not broken or fragmented during this process. Most of the fracturing occurred subsequently, when the sections were cut into smaller pieces. For the *mensef* meal, and also for many other meals, the meat is cut as follows: long bone sections and rib sections are cut into three or four small pieces; the scapula is cut into three or four pieces; vertebral column sections are frequently split right down the middle, cutting each vertebra into two or more pieces; the pelvis is usually split at the pubis into two parts; thereafter each part is chopped into three or four smaller pieces.

Table 4 shows the counts of skeletal remains from each of the four loci studied. The various elements are presented as members of the major sections of the animal, based on the above observations of butchering practices at the village of Ḥesbân. The total number of bones from each sample is shown at the bottom of the chart. To allow for quick reference to each sample in the subsequent discussion, note the abbreviations at the top of Table 4: H.1 and H.2 = Hellenistic samples from Loci D.1:59 and D.1:60; L.R.1 and L.R.2 = Late Roman samples from Loci D.2:36 and D.2:40.

In three of the four samples, skull fragments made up the largest group: H.1 = 31%, L.R.1 = 48%, L.R.2 = 37.5%. In H.2 skull fragments were outnumbered by vertebra fragments 28.5% to 18.6%. The very high percentage of skull fragments in L.R.1 is partially calculated from the large number of molars (separate from those in mandibles) found in that sample.

Mandible fragments were arranged into three types based on the portions of the bone most frequently recovered. A = ascending ramus, B = longitudinal ramus, C = front section. Ascending ramus fragments were most common in all the samples except in L.R.1, where front sections were more numerous.

On the whole, skull fragments were more common in the Late Roman samples than in the Hellenistic samples. Mandible fragments were more than twice as plentiful in the Late Roman as in the Hellenistic samples.

Vertebra fragments were categorized as follows: A = neural arch fragment, B = centrum, C = centrum epiphysis, D = spine, E = entire neural canal, F = complete, G = vertically split centrum. Vertebrae were very numerous in H.1 (20%) and H.2 (28.5%), while relatively few were found in L.R.1 (5.7%) and L.R.2 (5.3%). The fragments were mostly neural arch, spine, and centrum fragments. Four centrum fragments from the Hellenistic samples showed signs of having been split vertically (apparently as in the observed butchering practice). One such fragment was found in the Late Roman samples. Rib fragments were present only in the Hellenistic samples.

Pelvis fragments were grouped into eight categories: A = ilium with no evidence of pit, B = ischium with no evidence of acetabulum, C = pubis with no evidence of acetabulum, D = ilium with evidence of pit, E = ischium with evidence of aceta-

| SECTIONS | BONE | H.1 (D.1:59) | | | H.2 (D.1:60) | | | L.R.1 (D.2:36) | | | L.R.2 (D.2:40) | | |
|---|---|---|---|---|---|---|---|---|---|---|---|---|---|
| ABBREVIATIONS | | R | L | X | R | L | X | R | L | X | R | L | X |
| SKULL | MAXILLA | | | 4 | | | 1 | | | 1 | | | |
| | INCISOR | | | | | | | | | 1 | | | 2 |
| | PREMOLAR | | | 3 | | | 1 | | | 4 | | | 1 |
| | MOLAR | | | 11 | | | 2 | | | 39 | | | 8 |
| | MANDIBLE A | 3 | 3 | | 4 | 1 | | 4 | 4 | | 2 | 6 | |
| | " B | | 1 | | 1 | | 1 | 1 | | | 1 | 2 | 3 |
| | " C | 3 | | | | 1 | | 9 | 3 | | 1 | 2 | |
| | SKULL ? | | | 4 | | | 1 | | | | | | |
| VERTEBRAE | ATLAS | | | 1 | | | 2 | | | | | | |
| | AXIS | | | | | | 1 | | | | | | |
| | CERVICAL | | | 6 | | | 3 | | 2 | | | | 1 |
| | THORACIC | | | 7 | | | 9 | | 2 | | | | 2 |
| | LUMBAL | | | 3 | | | 1 | | 4 | | | | 1 |
| | SACRAL | | | 1 | | | | | | | | | |
| | VERTEBRAE ? | | | 3 | | | 4 | | | | | | |
| RIB CAGE | RIB | 1 | 1 | | 2 | 1 | | | | | | | |
| PELVIS | PELVIS A | | | | 1 | 1 | | 1 | | | | | |
| | " D | 1 | | | 2 | | | | | | | | |
| | " E | | | | 1 | | | | 3 | | 1 | 2 | |
| | " F | | | | | | | | | | 1 | 1 | |
| | " G | | | | | | | 1 | | | | | |
| FORELIMB | SCAPULA A | | 2 | | | 2 | | 1 | | | | | |
| | " B | 1 | 3 | 1 | | | | | | | | | |
| | " C | 2 | 1 | | | | | | | | | | |
| | " D | 1 | | | | | | | | | | | |
| | HUMERUS PR | 1 | 2 | | 1 | 2 | | 1 | 2 | | | | |
| | " SH | | | | | | 1 | | | | | | |
| | RADIUS PR | 2 | 1 | | 2 | | | 1 | | | 1 | | |
| | " DI | 1 | | | | 1 | | | 1 | | | | |
| | " SH | 2 | 1 | | | | 1 | 2 | 3 | 3 | | | |
| | ULNA | | | | | | | | | 1 | | | |
| HIND LIMB | FEMUR PR | | 1 | 3 | | | 2 | | 3 | | | | |
| | " DI | | | | | | | | | | | 1 | |
| | " SH | | 1 | | | | | 1 | | | | | |
| | TIBIA PR | | 1 | | 1 | | | | | | | | |
| | " DI | 3 | | | 1 | 1 | | 1 | | | | 2 | 1 |
| | " SH | | | 1 | | | | | | | | | |
| EXTREMITIES | METAPOD. | | | 1 | | | | | | | | | |
| | METACARP. PR | | 4 | | 1 | 1 | | 1 | 4 | 2 | 1 | 3 | 2 |
| | " DI | 1 | | 1 | | | 1 | | | 3 | | | 3 |
| | " SH | | | | | | | | | 2 | | | 3 |
| | METATARS. PR | | | 2 | 1 | | 1 | | 1 | 2 | 3 | 1 | 3 |
| | " DI | | | 1 | | | | | | 2 | | | 1 |
| | " SH | | | 1 | | | 1 | | | | | | 2 |
| | PHALANX I | 2 | 2 | | 1 | 2 | | 9 | 4 | | 4 | 3 | |
| | " II | 3 | | | | | | 3 | | | 2 | 3 | |
| | " III | | | | | | | 1 | | | 3 | 1 | |
| | TALUS | | | | 1 | 2 | | | | | | | |
| | CALCANEUS | | 1 | | 1 | 1 | | 3 | 1 | | | | |
| NUMBER OF BONES IN SAMPLE: | | 105 | | | 70 | | | 130 | | | 75 | | |

Table 4. Raw counts of skeletal remains of sheep and goats from four loci. Key: R = right side; L = left side; X = undifferentiated; PR = proximal end; DI = distal end; SH = shaft.

bulum, F = pubis with evidence of acetabulum, G = acetabulum with ilium and ischium, and H = obturator foramem with partial or complete acetabulum. Pelves were more common in the Late Roman samples where types E and F dominated. Types A and D dominated the Hellenistic samples.

Bones of the forelimb were more numerous in H.1 (20%) and H.2 (14.4%) than in L.R.1 (10.8%) and L.R.2 (1.3%). Scapula fragments were grouped into four types: A = blade with evidence of spine but no glenoid cavity, B = blade with no evidence of spine or glenoid cavity, C = evidence of glenoid cavity and spine, D = glenoid cavity only. Almost all the scapula fragments came from H.1. Only distal ends and shafts of humeri were represented. Radius fragments were best represented by shafts. Only one ulna fragment was found in L.R.1.

Bones of the hind limb were also more common in H.1 (8.5%) and H.2 (7.1%) than in L.R.1 (3.6%) and L.R.2 (5.4%). Femurs were mostly proximal end fragments, while tibia remains were mostly distal end fragments. Hind limb fragments, however, were fewer than forelimb fragments.

Extremities were numerous in all four samples. L.R.1 (26.7%) and L.R.2 (42.8%) had more than H.1 (17.9%) and H.2 (20%). Metacarpals were slightly more numerous than metatarsals. For all the metapodials, proximal ends were better represented than distal ends. First phalanges were by far the best represented; second and third phalanges followed far behind. Somehow right phalanges seem to outnumber left ones by quite a few. A few tali and calcanei were also found, mostly in H.2 and L.R.1.

In answering the question, "How were the bones fragmented?" it is now possible to suggest that they were, for the most part, fragmented as a result of butchering and meat cutting. The majority of the long bones were represented by either proximal ends, shafts, or distal ends; the scapula appears to have been cut into three or four pieces; the vertebral column shows signs of having been split down the middle; the pelvis was fragmented into eight or more sections. These fragment categories are strikingly similar to the fragment categories that resulted from the meat cutting observed at the present-day village.

There are signs indicating that the animals were slaughtered in close proximity to the dwellings rather than outside the village. Since fragments of skulls, except for the mandibles, and feet are frequently not saved, we would not expect to find many of them unless they were discarded within the village. During both periods, judging from the large number of these fragments found, it seems that they were so discarded in the village.

None of the distal ends of tibia show signs of having been pierced, a strong indication of butchershop practices whereby carcasses are hung on hooks by the distal tibia. This would suggest that the meat was not acquired in butcher shops.

There appear to have been at least four animals represented in each of the Hellenistic samples (four left distal tibiae, four right mandibles). The Late Roman bones appear to stem from a greater number of animals, at least nine right mandibles in L.R.1 and at least six left mandibles in L.R.2. There exists a greater discrepancy between right and left bones in the Late Roman samples than in the Hellenistic (see for example mandibles and phalanges).

Along with the above mentioned discrepancy between right and left bones, the Late Roman samples differ from the Hellenistic samples in other ways: There are very few vertebrae, no ribs, generally fewer fore- and hind-limbs, but numerous mandible fragments and extremities. No easy explanation for this problem has been found.

Finally it should be mentioned that the samples described above are probably biased somewhat by the identification skills of the authors. For example, proximal and distal ends of long bones are easier to identify than shafts, especially in the case of humeri and femurs. Other biases are likely accounted for by post-depositional effects: skull fragments are much less likely to endure considerable kicking around than are pelvis fragments.

In conclusion, from this preliminary study of 380 bone fragments the following summary statements can be made:

1. Sheep constituted a larger portion of the herds in the Hellenistic period than in the Late Roman period.

2. Females constituted a larger portion of the mature animals in both periods.

3. The animals were slaughtered at an earlier age in the Late Roman period than in the Hellenistic period.

4. The fragmentation of the animal bones appears to have resulted in large measure from meat-cutting practices during both periods.

5. The Late Roman animals may have been slightly larger than Hellenistic ones.

6. Late Roman fragments may have been generally larger than Hellenistic ones.

7. In both periods, the animals were slaughtered in close proximity to the villagers' dwellings.

8. For both periods, the evidence suggests that each family slaughtered and ate their own animals rather than having acquired them in butcher shops.

Futher study will be required to establish the integrity of these findings.

PLATE I

A. The staff of the 1973 Heshbon expedition. Photo: Avery V. Dick.

B. Fragment of the multicolored mosaic floor of the Byzantine church in Square A.5.
Photo: Avery V. Dick.

PLATE II

A. The opening of the furnace of the Islamic bath in Square A.7. Photo: Abu Hannah.

B. The inside of the furnace looking toward the horizontal flue which begins at the hole in the background. It heats the bathing room above. The edge of a black basalt slab is visible on which the floor tiles rest. Photo: Avery V. Dick.

PLATE III

A. The bathing room of the Islamic bath in Squares A.7 and 8. The meter stick lies on the tiled floor. To its left is Wall A.8:2 which contains the Chimney A.8:10. Photo: James H. Zachary.

B. The water basin of stone in the bathing room. Above the basin are the outlets for the hot water (left) and the cold water (right). Photo: Avery V. Dick.

PLATE IV

A. The header-stretcher Wall B.2:84 in Square B.2 which was probably the eastern retaining wall of a large open-air water basin. Note the remains of plaster at its southern end near the center in the picture. Photo: Avery V. Dick.

B. A one-meter square probe through the plaster at the bottom of Square B.1. Notice the three distinctive layers of plaster, each about 10 centimeters thick. The plaster layers rest on limestone bedrock which for control purposes was penetrated for ca. 30 centimeters to make sure bedrock was actually reached. Photo: James H. Zachary.

PLATE V

B. The possible Iron Age city Wall C.3:34/28 (in the lower left corner) and its Bastion C.3:32/26, jutting out to the west (above). The meter stick lies on the same bedrock on which the structures rest. Photo: Paul J. Bergsma.

A. The header-stretcher Wall B.2:84 can be seen above the left end of the meter stick. The latter rests on the balk. The continuation of Wall B.2:84 is seen in Square B.4. In the foreground is the large Rock B.4:168 with water channels carved into it. Photo: Paul J. Bergsma.

PLATE VI

A. Fragment of the Roman Tower C.1:40 in Square C:1. A later wall (C.1:30) abuts it on the right. Photo: Paul J. Bergsma.

B. The southern exterior wall (D.5:12 = D.6:55) of the Byzantine church is in the upper right part of the picture. Notice its doorway and arch over Cistern D.6:33. Flowing into the cistern from Catch Basin D.5:31 is Channel D.6:63. Channel D.5:20 flows in opposite direction toward Cistern D.5:5 (not shown in this picture). Wall D.6:56b runs to lower left. Photo: Paul J. Bergsma.

PLATE VII

A. Southern end of monumental Late Roman Stairway D.3:39. Excavation in lower left has gone below Surface D.3:44 associated with stairs to expose Wall D.3:47a at left and earthquake-damaged slabs of bedrock in center. Photo: Avery V. Dick.

B. Carved stone which originally had crowned the southern end of the balustrade of the Late Roman Stairway D.3:39. Photo: James H. Zachary.

PLATE VIII

B. Probe in south balk of Square D.1 showing the back of Wall D.2:21/26 battered up against Hellenistic soil layers which covered the artificially-cut shelf of bedrock on which the meter stick rests. The base of Wall D.1:4d is visible at bottom. Photo: James H. Zachary.

A. Water Channel D.1:58 = D.2:30 running from beneath gateway through Wall D.1:4c in the background to Stairway D.2:32 (on right), Stairs D.2:7b (on left), and Stairs D.2:34 (bottom left). Photo: Avery V. Dick.

PLATE IX

A. The stone shoring in the southeast corner of Tomb F.14. The shoring covers the openings to Loculi 3 and 4. Loculi 5 and 6 are visible at the left of the shoring. Photo: James H. Zachary.

B. Looking into Loculus 9 of Tomb F.14 which shows the break-through to Loculus 5 of Tomb F.18. Photo: Avery V. Dick.

PLATE X

A. Loculi 9-12 of Tomb F.18. Photo: Paul J. Bergsma.

B. Byzantine shaft Tombs F.15 (right) and F.17. Photo: Paul J. Bergsma.

PLATE XI

A. Roman milestones near *el Mushaqqar* (Grid Reference 2217.1342). Photo: Robert D. Ibach.

B. Roman milestones at *Serâbît Musshaqqar* (Grid Reference 2203.1341). Photo: Avery V. Dick.

PLATE XII

A. Cobble stones of the Roman road east of Site No. 35 (Grid Reference 2196.1341).
Photo: Avery V. Dick.

B. Dolmen at *Gourmeyet Hesbân* (Grid Reference 2252.1357). Photo: B. Charlene Hogsten.

PLATE XIII

A. A sector of the Roman road. It begins in the picture at the right (above the man's head) and goes toward the upper left until it is lost over the ridge. Photo: Avery V. Dick.

B. The remains of a square structure of Roman times, probably a road station. Photo: Avery V. Dick.

PLATE XIV

A. Roman and Byzantine glass vessels from Tombs F.16 and 18. Photo: Avery V. Dick.

B. Roman pottery from Tomb F.18. Photo: Avery V. Dick.

PLATE XV

A. Byzantine pottery from Tombs F.14 and 18. Photo: Avery V. Dick.

B. Islamic pottery from various loci on the *tell*. Photo: Avery V. Dick.

PLATE XVI

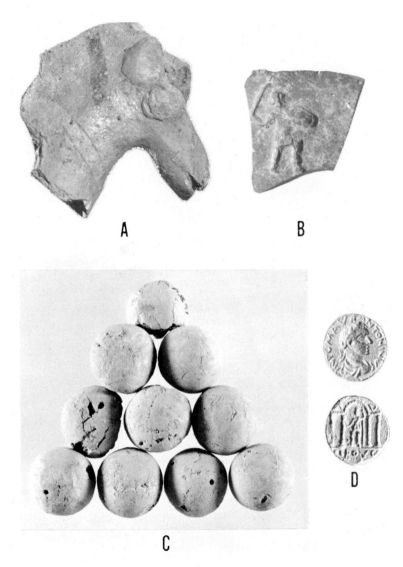

A
B
C
D

A. A painted terra cotta head of a horse of Iron II/Persian times found in Locus B.1:143. Photo: Paul J. Bergsma.

B. A Hellenistic sherd; the molded decoration shows a shield- and sword-bearing soldier; from Locus C.1:83. Photo: Paul J. Bergsma.

C. Some of the 15 Islamic clay marbles found in A.7. Photo: Eugenia L. Nitowski.

D. The Esbus coin of Elagabalus (A.D. 218-222) from Locus B.4:113. Photo: Eugenia L. Nitowski. (All objects are depicted actual size.)

# AMMONITE OSTRACA FROM HESHBON

## HESHBON OSTRACA IV-VIII

FRANK MOORE CROSS
Harvard University

The excavations at Heshbon in the summer of 1973 produced additional ostraca,[1] one of exceptional interest in an Ammonite cursive script (Ostracon IV), the others of relatively little value, a jar label in semi-formal Ammonite characters (Ostracon V), a sherd bearing a single crude 'alep (VI), and two ostraca on which the faint traces of ink are wholly illegible (VII, VIII).

### 1. Heshbon Ostracon IV (Fig. 1 and Pl. I)

Ostracon IV, Registry No. 1657, was found July 31, 1973, in Area B, Square 1, Locus 143, a context described by the excavator as Iron II/Persian. The upper-left side of the sherd is missing and with it the ends of the first seven lines of script, certainly, and perhaps the first eight. The right margin is intact except for a small chip at the very beginning of line 1, where at most a single letter is missing. Both the top and bottom seem to be the original line of breakage save for minor chips. The piece of pottery is a body sherd taken from a large, fairly rough storage jar. Its surface

---

[1] Ostraca found in earlier seasons (from the pre-Islamic period) at Heshbon include Ostracon I (309) and II (803), both written in the standard Aramaic cursive of the Persian chancellery dating to the end of the sixth century. One notes that the changeover from the national script to the standard Aramaic cursive takes place about the same time—the late sixth century—in Ammon and in Israel. The two ostraca above were published by the writer in *AUSS*, 7 (1969): 223-229; and in *AUSS*, 11 (1973): 126-131.

Abbreviations used in this article, but not listed on the back cover, are the following:

CTA      = Andrée Herdner, *Corpus des tablettes en cunéiformes alphabetiques* (Paris, 1963).

Gordon   = C. H. Gordon, *Ugaritic Manual* (Rome, 1955).

PRU     = Claude F.-A. Schaeffer, *Le palais royal d'Ugarit* (Paris, 1955-1970).

*Ugaritica V* = Jean Nougayrol, et al., *Ugaritica V* (Paris, 1968).

is not always smooth and frequently contains large calcium grits. The scribe's pen strokes in consequence are broad and sometimes distorted by unevenness or blurred by the spread of the ink. Nevertheless, given sufficient effort, most of the letters in the eleven lines of the inscription can be made out.

The text of the ostracon reads as follows:

1. *[l]mlk. 'kl 20+10+5* (?)[                                    ]
2. *wṣ'n 8* (VACAT)                    [                        ]
3. *wlndb'l bn n'm'l m*[                                        ]
4. *lz*[    ]*m'lt nk't 10+2 ' k̄* [*l*                          ]
5. *l*[    ] *nk't 2 'rḥ bt 2 w*[                                ]
6. *lb'š['] ksp 20+20 'š ntn l*[                                ]
7. *yn 20+2 wṣ'n 10 lbbt* [                                    ]
8. *yn 8 w'kl 6*
9. *lytb dš̌ 'kl 20+4* (?)
10. *ṣ'n 9*
11. *'rḥ bt 3*

1. To the king: 35 (jars) of grain [                          ]
2. and 8 small cattle.                    [                      ]
3. and to Nadab'el son of Na'am'el from [                      ]
4. To Z[    ] from Elath: 12 (measures) of gum; g[rain        ]
5. To [    ] 2 (measures) of gum; a two-year old cow and
   [    ]
6. To Ba'ash[a] 40 (pieces) of silver which he gave to [    ]
7. 22 (bottles) of wine; and 10 small cattle; fine flour [    ]
8. 8 (bottles) of wine; and six (jars) of grain.
9. To Yatib hay; 24 (jars) of grain;
10. 9 small cattle;
11. a three-year-old cow.

Line 1. The reconstruction *[l]mlk* is virtually certain. There is room for one letter only at the beginning of the line. A personal name with *l* (as elsewhere in the inscription), e.g. *['l]mlk,* cannot be fitted into the space.

Fig. 1. A tracing of the Heshbon Ostracon IV.

We have translated '*kl* "grain." Often '*ōkel* refers to a cereal in the Bible, and at Ugarit, as D. R. Hillers has shown, '*akl* evidently means "grain" or even "flour."[2] Thus it is used in *CTA* (KRT), 14.18, 172 where the parallel term is *ḥṭṭ* "wheat." More important for our context is the reference in an economic text: '*arb'm dd 'akl*,

[2] "An Alphabetic Cuneiform Tablet from Taanach (TT 433)," *BASOR*, No. 173 (Feb., 1964): 49.

"forty jars of grain."[3] To these references may be added probably the Canaanite cuneiform tablet from Taanach: "Kôkaba' (meted out) to Pu'm, 8 *kprt* (vessels) of sifted grain (*'akl dk*)." [4] Akkadian *akalu and aklu* have developed similar specialized meanings: "bread" and "barley" (or barley products). Canaanite *laḥmu*, "food" follows a similar pattern of semantic development, coming to mean in Hebrew "bread."

The number at the end of line 1 is quite uncertain after the sign for "twenty." The upper-left corner is badly chipped.

Line 2. The vacant space at the end of this line suggests that the list of stores assigned to the crown ends here.

Line 3. The name *Nadab'el* is a popular one in Ammon. Vattioni lists three occurrences on Ammonite seals.[5] Nachman Avigad has published a fourth.[6] *Na'am'el* appears elsewhere on a Punic seal,[7] and the element *n'm* is extremely common in Canaanite onomastica, including Ugaritic, Phoenician, and Hebrew.

We have read the final letter as *m* before the break. Presumably the home town of Nadab'el followed (as is the case in line 4: *m'lt*, "from Elath"), and then the commodity and amount. It is interesting that the most common name alone in the text is specified further by both patronymic and place of origin.

Line 4. The initial *zayin* of the personal name expected is all that can be read. Following it is a large blemish which may or may not have contained a letter. After the blemish, traces of ink are discernible but indecipherable.

---

[3] Gordon, 1126.3, 4 (*PRU*, II, 126.3, 4).

[4] The reading follows Hillers (see note 2) for the most part, and goes against the writer's earlier proposals, "The Canaanite Cuneiform Tablet from Taanach," *BASOR*, No. 190 (April, 1968): 41-46. Incidentally, the forms *kprt* and Akk. *karpatu* "earthenware vessel" (esp. of standard measure) are probably cognates.

[5] F. Vattioni, "I sigilli ebraici," *Biblica*, 50 (1969): 357-388: Nos. 29,1; 159,2; 201,1. The seal listed as 159 was attributed to Hebron by Reifenberg, but to judge from its script is Ammonite in origin.

[6] "Ammonite and Moabite Seals," *Near Eastern Archaeology in the Twentieth Century*, ed. J. A. Sanders (New York, 1970), pp. 284-295, esp. p. 288 and Pl. 30, 4.

[7] Vattioni, *Biblica*, 50 (1969), No. 95, 1.

The appearance of the term *nk't* in lines 4 and 5 apparently guarantees the reading. The initial letter in each instance could be *nūn or mêm*. I was first tempted to read *mr't* "fatlings" in line 5; however, the second letter is certainly *kap* in line 4, and most easily is read *kap* in line 5. We have translated "gum." In Hebrew the term is *nk't*, vocalized *nᵉkôt*. It appears as an item of merchandise along with balsam and ladanum brought by camel caravan from Gilead;[8] in its only other occurrence in the Bible it is in a list of gifts to be brought from Palestine to Egypt: balm, honey, gum, ladanum, pistachio nuts and almonds.[9] The term may be cognate with Akkadian *nukātu* (*nukkatu*) and with Arabic *nuka'at*, a byform of *nuka'at* and *naka'at*, gum of tragacanth, an aromatic resin from the shrub *Astragalus gummifer* and *Astragalus tragacantha*, used in food and medicine.

The writing *'lt* for Elath, the port on the Gulf of Aqabah, is that expected. The name probably derives from the goddess' name, [*Bêt*] *'Ēlat;* the alternate etymology suggested, from *'yl(t)*, "terebinth," whether derived from *\*'ilatu* or *\*'aylatu* (> *\*'êlatu*) would have been written *'lt* in the Ammonite of this period.

The word following the number begins with *'alep*. The following traces fit best with *kap: 'k[l(?)]*, "grain."

Line 5. We can assume that after the initial *l* came a personal name. The traces of ink have virtually disappeared. The second letter of the name, the third after *lameḏ*, is best preserved; the traces appear to fit *'alep*. *Šīn* may follow giving *l[y]'š* "to Yā'ōš."[10]

At the end of line 5 we find the sequence *'rḥ bt 2*, and in line 11 *'rḥ bt 3*. We take *'rḥ* as identical with Ugaritic *'arḥ* (plural *'arḫt*) "young cow," Akk. *arḫu* "cow," Arab. *'arḫu* "young bull," *'arḫat* "heifer." The following *bt 2* in line 5, *bt 3* in line 11, are abbreviated forms of *bat šᵉnātayim* and *bat šālōš šānōt*[11] respec-

---

[8] Gn 37:25.

[9] Gn 43:11.

[10] On this name and others from the same root, see F. M. Cross, "An Aramaic Inscription from Daskyleion," *BASOR*, No. 184 (Dec., 1966): 8, n. 17.

[11] Cf. the Ammonite *bšnt rḥqt* "in years far off" in the Tell Sīrān Bronze

tively, "two years old" and "three years old." One may compare
the biblical expressions *bt šnth* and *bn šntw* "one year old" used
of sacrificial animals, Ugaritic *ʻglm dt šnt,* "calves a year old";[12]
and also *ʻglt mšlšt,* "a three-year-old cow"[13] and *pr mšlš,* a three-
year-old bull."[14] It appears that in antiquity cows aged two or
three years were considered ideal for slaughter.[15]

Line 6. The name *Baʻašaʼ,* in addition to its appearance as a
royal name in Israel, was the name of an Ammonite king of the
ninth century B.C. who fought at Qarqar:[16]

The phrase *ʼš ntn l-* is useful in drawing Canaanite isoglosses.
The relative *ʼš* ( *<ša*) stands with Phoenician and North Israelite
versus Hebrew and Moabite *ʼašer. Ntn,* however, sides with
Moabite,[17] North Israelite, and Hebrew *ntn* versus the new
formation *ytn* in Phoenician and North Canaanite.

Line 7. The spelling *yn* here and in line 8 indicates the con-
traction of the diphthong *ay > ê* as in Ugaritic, Phoenician, and
North Israelite. The writing *bn ʻmn* in the Tell Sīrān Bronze may
confirm: *banê ʻammōn.*[18]

The word *lbbt* obviously is related to biblical *lĕbībōt,* usually
translated "cakes" or "pancakes." In Arabic *libābat* means "fine
flour," and the derivation of the meaning is clear: "inner part,"
hence "choice part." Similarly in Syriac starch is called *lebbā*
*de-ḥeṭṭātāʼ,* "the heart of wheat." Hebrew *lĕbībōt,* "cakes" then

---

discussed by the writer in his paper "Notes on the Ammonite Inscription
from Tell Sīrān," *BASOR,* No. 212 (Dec., 1973): 12-15.

[12] *CTA,* 22.2.13 (*Gordon,* 124); 4.6.43 (*Gordon,* 51).

[13] Gn 15:9.

[14] 1 Sa 1:24 (according to 4QSamᵃ and the Old Greek).

[15] In an Akkadian text cited in *The Assyrian Dictionary,* I, A, Part II
(Chicago, 1968), p. 263, a buyer is prepared to pay silver for "cows either
three-year-old or two-year-old ones" (ÁB.ḪI.A [*arḫātim*] *šumma* MU 3 *šumma*
*šaddidātim*).

[16] D. D. Luckenbill, *Ancient Records of Assyria and Babylonia,* 1 (Chicago,
1926): 611. The name is written *ba-ʼ-sa* as expected.

[17] Cf. the Moabite name *kmšntn* on a seal published by Avigad, "Ammonite
and Moabite Seals" (see n. 6 above), p. 290.

[18] It is possible also to read the old plural oblique *banī* (ʻAmmōn). Note
also the writing *ywmt* "days."

are named from their content (not their shape!), the special flour from which they are made. In the present context clearly "fine flour" is a more suitable translation than "cakes" or "loaves."

Line 9. The name *ytb* may be a hypocoristicon of such Canaanite names as *'strty[t]b* or *ytb'l* hitherto explained as errors or by-forms of *ytn*. In Thamudic there is a name *ytb*, probably a G or causative imperfect of *wtb*: Yatib.[19]

The word *déše'*, "grass," "hay" may be followed by a number; if so, it can be only one or two strokes. There is too little room even for the symbol "10." It may be that the rough amount of hay supplied was known, or was not worth measuring out precisely, and hence no number was recorded.

The list is most easily interpreted as the record kept by a royal steward of the assignment or distribution from the royal stores of foodstuffs, beef and mutton, grain and wine, as well as money and spicery, to the personal household of the king, to courtiers, and to others to whom the crown was under obligation. Since the king is first named, and food, grain, and mutton, in sizable amounts is then listed, we must assume that the king is a recipient. The king does not pay taxes in kind. The other persons named, therefore, are also recipients of the designated items rather than the names of men credited with taxes in kind sent to the royal stores.

This text so understood is paralleled by many economic texts listing the distribution of food stuffs and various other commodities under the formula *l* + PN. A number of such texts are known from Ugarit.[20] One may compare also the Ta'anach Tablet

[19] Cf. G. Ryckmans, *Les noms propres sud-sémitiques,* 1 (Louvain, 1934): 213, who suggests the root *tbb* perhaps found in Safaitic *tbn* as well. The root *wtb*, "to rest," "sojourn" seems preferable. The root *tbb* means basically "to do harm" or "to suffer harm or loss." To be sure *tābb* cited by Ryckmans can mean "strong"; it also means "feeble" or "weak," the familiar phenomenon of *didd* (contrary/similar). Arabic *twb* is not a candidate, being a late Aramaic loanword, cognate with *twb* > *šwb* in Canaanite.

[20] *PRU* 2: 88-101 (*Gordon,* 1088-1101, of which 1098 may be an inventory of royal stores); *PRU* 5: 12-13; *Ugaritica V,* 99-100. The closest parallels are *PRU* 2: 89, 90. A. F. Rainey has collected and discussed some of these and

described above, and more remotely the Tell Qasileh ostracon: *zhb. 'pr. lbyt ḥrn š 10+10+10*, "Gold of Ophir, presented (*ex voto*) to the Temple of Hôrôn."[21] In the El Kôm Ostraca, Qôsyada' the moneylender notes loans *to* a person by *l* + PN, money received in repayment *from mn* + PN.[22]

If we follow the theory of Aharoni and Rainey, the Samaria ostraca also note distribution of goods from the royal storehouse to officers of the king.[23] However, the Samaria Ostraca present very special problems. I am inclined to regard them as tax receipts. They come from the royal storehouse in the citadel of Samaria and appear now to date in the reign of Jeroboam II in the years 774 to 778.[24] The ostraca contain two groups of men,

other texts attempting to demonstrate that *l* + PN can be used of "recipients," as well as of "owners." I have no doubt he is correct. Indeed *l-* can mean "belonging to," "product of," "distributed to," "credited to," "lent to," "presented" or "given to" in extant epigraphic material. However, I cannot follow Rainey in his interpretation (shared with Aharoni) of the Samaria Ostraca. Cf. A. F. Rainey, "Administration in Ugarit and the Samaria Ostraca," *IEJ*, 12 (1962): 62f.; "The Samaria Ostraca in the Light of Fresh Evidence," *PEQ*, 99 (1967): 32-41; "A Hebrew 'Receipt' from Arad," *BASOR*, No. 202 (April, 1971): 23-29.

[21] Published by B. Maisler (Mazar), "The Excavations at Tell Qasîle," *IEJ*, 1 (1950-51): 194-252, esp. pp. 208ff. and Pls. 37A, 38A.

[22] The ostraca, including a bilingual in Greek and Edomite are to be published by L. T. Geraty in the near future.

[23] See Y. Aharoni, *The Land of the Bible* (Philadelphia, 1967), pp. 315-327; and above n. 20 for reference to Rainey's papers.

[24] This seems certain now, thanks to Aharoni's definitive solution of the Samaria numerals: "The Use of Hieratic Numerals in Hebrew Ostraca and the Shekel Weights," *BASOR*, No. 184 (Dec., 1966): 13-19, confirmed by Ivan Kaufman, "New Evidence for Hieratic Numerals on Hebrew Weights," *BASOR*, No. 188 (Dec., 1967): 39-41. It is difficult to separate the two groups, 9th- and 10th-year ostraca on the one side, 15th-year ostraca on the other. The script is remarkably homogeneous. Yet it is strange that there is not clear overlap of names. However, if we were inclined to attribute the two groups to two different kings, we should have to reduce the 9th- and 10th-year group to the last years of Menahem (738, 737), rather than raise their dates to a time before Jeroboam II. The script is very far developed even for the reign of Jeroboam. Cf. my remarks, *BASOR*, No. 165 (Febr., 1962): 34-42, where I followed Yadin's suggested interpretation of the numerals. The raising of the date of the Samaria Ostraca suggests that the Murabba'āt Papyrus be raised to ca. 700 (my former date was 700-650 B.C.), and associated with the Assyrian crisis in Hezekiah's reign.

"*l*-men" (whose name is preceded by the preposition *l*) and "non-*l*-men." The "*l*-men" repeat, indeed eight of the dozen "*l*-men" appear in the ostraca more than once. Gaddiyaw turns up eight times, 'Ašā' eight times. Moreover, the "*l*-men" are associated frequently with more than one place or clan. The name 'Ašā' on ostraca with commodities coming from 'Abi'ezer, Šemīda' and Ḥeleq. Indeed the place names specify the origin of oil or wine and may precede or follow the "*l*-man"; on the contrary, a place name may identify a "non-*l*-man" (always following when given). The "non-*l*-men" generally are specified more carefully, often with patronymic, gentilic, or town of origin. They never repeat except with the same "*l*-man," the same district and/or town. In Ostraca 1 and 2 several "non-*l*-men" are listed with the numerals 1 or 2 (jars) following their name. When one (rarely two) jars only are in a shipment, one "non-*l*-man" is named or none is named.

From these data we can make several inferences: (1) "*l*-men" are not tax officials unless one assumes administrative chaos with overlapping districts; (2) "non-*l*-men" are small men, attached, unlike the "*l*-men," to one place or estate and to one "*l*-man," and hence are tenants, sharecroppers, or the like, who actually bring commodities to the royal storehouse; (3) the small quantity in the shipments suggests that we have to do not with royal estates or with the total produce of an estate, royal or private.

If these inferences are sound, I believe we must opt for the explanation that most of the ostraca are tax receipts. This fits with the small amount in shipments. If the documents were inventories of produce of royal estates, the number would be far larger; if the documents recorded rations given to a courtier or noble from the storehouse we should expect higher numbers and more than one (or two) commodities listed. Here we may compare our Heshbon Ostracon. It does not seem likely either that the Samaria ostraca record the produce of lands given by royal grant to favored officials. Such produce would go directly to the owner without going through the royal storehouses, and the produce would be far greater in quantity.

However, if we explain the ostraca as tax receipts, their form and content can be comprehended. The shipments come from the estates of landed (military) nobility[25] which are widely distributed, and are not hereditary lands since one man owns estates in as many as three clans. The "non-*l*-men" are tenants, clients, etc., attached to an individual estate, who bring the appropriate tax in kind to the royal storehouse to be credited to the account of their lords, the "*l*-men." Hence the transaction is properly recorded with an official date of receipt. The district (clan, village, or estate) is listed precisely or imprecisely since the district in question identifies the quality of the product, especially in the case of aged wine. The listing of the "non-*l*-man" more precisely identified usually than the better-known "*l*-men," gives proof that he delivered the wine or oil. We assume that copies of the tax docket were returned to the estate owner as proof of delivery and payment of tax. The omission of the name of a "non-*l*-man" on receipts of a single jar or two is understandable, too, since the receipt is proof enough of his full delivery in such a case.[26]

The script of the Heshbon List is of great interest providing an additional cursive exemplar to our small corpus of Ammonite scripts. The earliest Ammonite document, the ʿAmmān Citadel Inscription, is inscribed in an Aramaic script of ca 850 B.C.[27] Sometime after the ʿAmmān Citadel text, and before the date of the Deir ʿAllā Texts,[28] Ammonite script diverged from its ancestral

---

[25] That is, *gibborê ḥayil*. The breakdown of the egalitarian land system of Israel came with the rise of a royal officialdom including commercial and military officers attached to the crown, who were rewarded with grants of land, fiefs. Cf. Y. Yadin, "Recipients or Owners, A Note on the Samaria Ostraca," *IEJ*, 9 (1959): 184-187; and especially "Ancient Judaean Weights and the Date of the Samaria Ostraca," *Scripta hierosolymitana*, 8 (1961): 22-25.

[26] On the use of *lmlk* on wine jars and *l* + PN on wine jars, see my remarks in the paper, "Jar Inscriptions from Shiqmona," *IEJ*, 18 (1968): 226-233. Neither are proper parallels to the usage of the Heshbon list.

[27] See my discussion, "Epigraphic Notes on the Ammān Citadel Inscription," *BASOR*, No. 193 (Feb., 1969): 13-19.

[28] H. J. Franken, "Texts from the Persian Period from Tell Deir ʿAllā," *VT*,

Aramaic and slowly began its own peculiar development.[29] The date of the Deir ʿAllā script is in dispute. Joseph Naveh, before the appearance of the new Ammonite texts, dated it on the basis of the related Aramaic sequence of scripts to the mid-eighth century B.C. or earlier.[30] Among others, the late Paul Lapp protested that the stratigraphy of Tell Deir ʿAllā did not permit so early a date, and noted that the floors of the building whose walls bore the inscriptions did contain Persian pottery.[31] The discovery of the Tell Sīrān Bronze made clear once and for all that Ammonite scribes did develop a national script style and happily provided a precise date with which to pin down its typological sequence date: ca. 600 B.C. or slightly later, in the reign of ʿAmmīnadab III, the great-great-grandson of that ʿAmmīnadab who was a contemporary of Assurbanipal. A monumental inscription on stone taken from the ruins of the ʿAmmān Theater comes from about the same date or slightly later.[32] Only two lines are preserved:

]bʿl. ʾbn ⌐h̄⌐ [
]bn ʿm[n]
]Baʿl. I shall build[
]the people of Ammon[

The Baʿl of the first line may well be a divine epithet or the name of the Ammonite king, preserved in corrupt form in Jer 40:14: bʿlys mlk bny ʿmn.[33] The second line contains the spelling of bn

17 (1967): 480f.

[29] Compare my earlier comments, "Notes on the Ammonite Inscription from Tell Sīrān," BASOR, No. 212 (Dec. 1973): 12-15.

[30] I followed Naveh (IEJ, 17 [1967]: 256-258) in this dating at the time he wrote, with the following caveat: "One should note, however, that the text shares certain idiosyncrasies with the later Ammonite and Moabite scripts on seals. It is not impossible, therefore, that it is diverging from the standard Aramaic cursive, and hence may preserve archaic forms beyond their time" (BASOR, No. 193 [Feb., 1969]: 14, n. 2).

[31] Paul W. Lapp, "The Tell Deir ʿAllā Challenge to Palestinian Archaeology," VT, 20 (1970), 255.

[32] R. W. Dajani, "The Ammon Theater Fragment," ADAJ, 12-13 (1967-68): 65ff.

[33] The samek may be a dittography of the following mêm in a MS of roughly the second century B.C. when samek and mêm were frequently confused.

'*m[n]* used throughout the Tell Sīrān text.[34] Thus on palaeo-
graphic and internal grounds the inscription would date to ca.
580 B.C. These new palaeographical data, plus the evidence of the
Heshbon List, require the lowering of the date of the Deir
'Allā Inscriptions to the early seventh century B.C.[35] The dating
to the early or middle eighth century rather identifies the time
when the Ammonite national script style broke free from the
main line of evolution of the standard Aramaic cursive and
lapidary styles—in the early eighth century. Among the chief
traits of the Ammonite script is its preservation of archaic forms:
*bêt, dalet, rêš,* and *'ayin* continue closed at the top, *dalet* and
*rêš* into the sixth century; other archaic features include the
complex *zayin* and *yōd* (into the sixth century), long-tailed *mêm*
with zigzag top, and the two-barred *ḥet*. At the same time certain
letters evolve in unique ways; most striking is the *hē* of the Tell
Sīrān Inscription.

Additional control of Ammonite writing styles is found in the
corpus of Ammonite seals which now can be isolated. The task
has been well begun by N. Avigad in his paper "Ammonite and
Moabite Seals."[36] Five seals can be narrowly dated: The two
seals of "servants of 'Ammīnadab" are dated by the king's reign to
the mid-seventh century B.C.,[37] two seals found in the tomb of

*Ba'lay* or simply *Ba'l* are well-known hypocoristica. However, a full form, on
the pattern of [*Zakar-*]*ba'l*, may have been put into a formal text. Alternately
we may take *b'lys* to be a textual corruption of *dblbs* found on the seal of
'*mnwt 'mt dblbs*. We expect '*mt* like '*bd* to be a royal title; similarly the
*ḥnn'l* of the seal of '*lyh 'mt ḥnn'l* may be the missing king in the dynasty of
Amminadab, the son of Amminadab I who flourished ca. 625 B.C. Cf. G. M.
Landes, "The Material Civilization of the Ammonites," *The Biblical Archaeologist Reader,* ed. E. F. Campbell and D. N. Freedman, 2 (Garden City, N.Y.,
1964): 85 and references.

[34] In the 'Ammān Citadel Inscription, the sequence in line 6

]*h. tšt'. bbn. 'lm* VACAT[

must be read in light of this orthography in the Tell Sīrān Text:

"you are feared among the gods."

[35] Evidently the building of the wall on which the inscriptions were penned
(or painted) was built in the seventh century at the beginning of new occupation and continued in use into the Persian period.

[36] See above, n. 6.

[37] Cf. G. R. Driver, "Seals and Tombstones," *ADAJ,* 2 (1953): Pl. VIII,

'Adōnīnūr 'Ammīnadab's official (*'abd*), one of *šūb'ēl*, and one of *menahēm ben yenahēm*,[38] and finally the seal of *byd'l 'bd pd'l*, long overlooked, dating to ca. 700.[39] These formal scripts of the seventh century are marked by great conservatism, extremely vertical stances, of which the *pe* is particularly remarkable, and certain innovations which are surprising: a square-shaped *'ayin*, long-legged *dalet* in vertical stance, the head of *mêm* with its zigzags in the form of a "w." Highly archaic are the forms of *'alep* (unchanged from the early eighth-century Aramaic forms), *yōd*, *bêt*, two-bar *het* (becoming a single bar in some sixth-century seal scripts), and angular *lamed*.

Pressures of the cursive on the formal and semi-formal (Tell Sīrān Bronze) styles introduce several changes toward 500 B.C.: *bêt* opens at the top, and sometimes *'ayin*; *hêt* may be reduced as noted above; *yōd* is elongated; *samek* exhibits a "z"-form head, *qōp* opens at the top. Several of these changes are found too in the Aramaic cursive and argillary[40] scripts. It must be emphasized, however, that the opening of *bêt* and *'ayin*, *dalet* and *rêš*, and the simplification to the one-bar *hêt* had taken place in Aramaic cursive scripts already by the end of the eighth century B.C., long before the Ammonite changes. In the Nimrud Ostracon, for example, of the late eighth century B.C. these changes are fully developed, and in the Assur Ostracon of ca. 660-650 B.C. there is no remnant of the archaic forms. Indeed Ammonite differs radically from the Aramaic in that *dalet* and *rêš* are not open normally in the latest Ammonite cursive, and archaic forms of

---

1-3; for the *'dnplt* seal, see A. Reifenberg, *Ancient Hebrew Seals* (London, 1950), p. 42, No. 35.

[38] N. Avigad, "An Ammonite Seal," *IEJ*, 2 (1952): 163f.

[39] *CIS*, 2: 76. See the writer's forthcoming study on the seal and its date. The king in question is ᵐPu-du-AN/*Pĕdō'ēl*/, who paid tribute to Sennacherib in 701 B.C. The Statue Inscription of *yrh'zr* is too crude and difficult to be of great help to the palaeographer; cf. B. D. Barnett, "Four Sculptures from Amman," *ADAJ*, 1 (1951): 34-36; Pl. XIII.

[40] See the discussion and script charts of Stephen J. Lieberman, "The Aramaic Argillary Script in the Seventh Century," *BASOR*, No. 192 (Dec., 1968): 25-31.

closed *ʿayin* persist to the end. At the same time it may be that some of the Ammonite changes took place under secondary Aramaic influence. No doubt Aramaic was known and its script read in Ammon in these centuries.

At present our latest texts in Ammonite script date clearly from the mid-sixth century B.C. From the very end of the sixth century come the Heshbon Ostraca I and II, both written in Aramaic script. So far as the evidence goes it fits with other data suggesting the general replacement of the old national scripts, Edomite, Ammonite, and Hebrew, by the Aramaic script universally used in the Persian chancelleries.[41] To be sure in narrow circles in Judaea and Samaria the old national script survived, becoming what we have labeled Palaeo-Hebrew; and similar survivals elsewhere, of which we as yet have no examples, may have existed.

Some brief comments can be made on the script of the Heshbon Ostracon IV in the context of the evolution of the Ammonite character.

*'Alep* in the Deir ʿAllā and Tell Sīrān scripts, as in the seventh-century seal scripts, retains its traditional eighth-century form showing little or no change. In the Heshbon *'alep*, the mode of penning has changed: the right two bars are made in a check or "v" motion; the left bar is made independently. The form is reminiscent of the "star" *'alep* of the argillary Aramaic script and the seventh-century forms in the Assur Ostracon and the Saqqarah Papyrus, but is not identical. Certainly it is typologically the most advanced of the *'aleps* in Ammonite.

*Bêṭ* in the Heshbon List is open at the top. In this it shows the developed tendency also at work in the more formal script of the Tell Sīrān Bronze. The cursive of Deir ʿAllā preserves the

<hr>

[41] Cf. the writer's comments and references in "Two Notes on the Palestinian Inscriptions of the Persian Age," *BASOR*, No. 193 (Feb., 1969): 32; an alternate view has been expressed by J. Naveh, "The Scripts in Palestine and Transjordan in the Iron Age," *Near Eastern Archaeology in the Twentieth Century*, ed. J. A. Sanders, pp. 277-281; and "Hebrew Texts in Aramaic Script in the Persian Period," *BASOR*, No. 203 (Oct., 1971): 27-32.

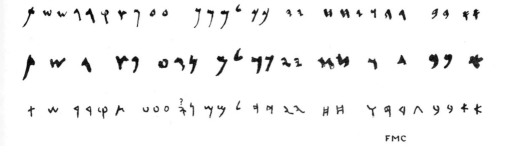

FMC

Fig. 2. Ammonite alphabets.

Line 1. The cursive script of the *Deir 'Allā* inscriptions from the early seventh century B.C.

Line 2. Heshbon Ostracon IV. Dating to the end of the seventh or to the beginning of the sixth century B.C. (In cursive script).

Line 3. The *Tell Sīrān* bronze inscription from the beginning of the sixth century B.C. (Engraved in a semifinal hand).

older, closed form.

*Dalet* and *rêš* in the Heshbon List reveal little or no tendency toward opening at the top. In the Tell Sīrān Inscription, one *dalet is* slightly open but it is clear that the standard form is closed. These letters stand in strongest opposition to the Aramaic type sequence and leave no doubt of the independence of the Ammonite alphabet over considerable periods of time. In the formal script and in the Deir 'Allā cursive the *dalet* tends to be greatly elongated.

The letter *hê* does not appear, unfortunately, in the Heshbon List. The Deir 'Allā form superficially resembles the simplified cursive *hê* of Aramaic, but two-bar forms and the extraordinary divided-rectangle of the head of the Tell Sīrān *hê* underline its peculiarity.

The *waw* of our Heshbon Ostracon follows precisely in the tradition of the Deir 'Allā *waw*, which parallels the Aramaic *waw*. The Tell Sīrān *waw* echoes a lapidary tradition found elsewhere in the archaizing lapidary scripts from Nerab (early seventh century B.C.). The form is not known in the main sequences of Aramaic formal and cursive scripts.

Both in the Deir 'Allā text and in the Tell Sīrān text, *ḥeṭ* preserves the older two-bar form of the early Aramaic scripts. The Heshbon List again displays the most developed letter form, with one bar. At the same time its ancestor is the type of *ḥeṭ* developed in the Ammonite tradition of Deir 'Allā, as opposed to the main Aramaic stream.

A formal *yōḏ* persists throughout the main line of Ammonite scripts. Simplification under Aramaic influence may be seen in the seal of *'byḥy bn ynḥm*.[42] The Tell Sīrān *yōḏ* shows a tendency to narrow and elongate.

The tradition of *kap* made with a triangular bar on the top left continues from Deir 'Allā through the Heshbon List. The older, lapidary *kap* appears in seventh century seal scripts. In Aramaic the form occurs sporadically in eighth and seventh century scripts, but never so stylized as in the Tell Sīrān script.

*Mêm* in the Deir 'Allā texts preserves the long lines and shallow, zigzag head of eighth-century Aramaic *mêm*. Throughout the Ammonite scripts we find no evidence of the Aramaic *mêm* developed in the seventh century with a vertical cross-bar cutting the head.

The letter *samek* is problematical in the Ammonite script. It appears to share a "z"-headed form with the argillary Aramaic scripts of the seventh century, and appears sporadically in lapidary texts, including Nerab. Unhappily, however, the Tell Sīrān *samek* is in dispute and the Heshbon *samek* is badly preserved.

'*Ayin* in the Ammonite cursive is round, in the Ammonite lapidary is square. The two occurrences in the Heshbon List are

[42] A. Reifenberg, *Ancient Hebrew Seals*, No. 40; cf. N. Avigad, "An Ammonite Seal," *IEJ*, 2 (1952): 164, n. 2.

closed or virtually closed. Some (but not all) of the ʿayins of the Tell Sīrān script are left open.

Pē is rounded at its top in Ammonite and tends more to the vertical than in the kindred Aramaic scripts of the seventh-sixth century.

Qōp retains more or less its archaic form in Ammonite, opening at the top but not developing the horizontal "s" top of the Aramaic cursive and argillary scripts of the seventh century B.C.

Šīn shows little development from ninth-eighth century forms.

Taw in the Deir ʿAllā texts and in the Tell Sīrān script derives directly from the elongated taw of ninth-eighth century Aramaic. In the Heshbon list the cross-bar has moved off to the right, a tendency already developed in seventh-century Aramaic.

The script of the Heshbon list shows itself more advanced than the Tell Sīrān script in the case of ʾalep, ḥêt, kap, samek and taw. Despite its highly cursive style as opposed to the semi-formal style of the Tell Sīrān inscription, its forms of ʿayin and yōd are less developed. In view of the great distance between the cursive of Deir ʿAllā and the cursive of Heshbon, it is difficult to date the Heshbon List earlier than the end of the seventh century B.C., two scribal generations after the Deir ʿAllā inscriptions. In view of internal historical data, the Tell Sīrān Bronze cannot be lowered much below 600 B.C., in no case later than 580 B.C. These data suggest that the Heshbon list is roughly contemporary with the Tell Sīrān Bronze, from the late seventh or early sixth century.

The language of the Heshbon Ostracon IV adds to the evidence that Ammonite was a South Canaanite dialect closely related to Phoenician, the Hebrew of Northern Israel, and in some features with Hebrew and Moabite.

Such a conclusion was already adumbrated by the evidence of Ammonite seals, and their use of characteristic Canaanite elements: bn, bt, nʿr, and ʾmt. The names on seals and in the texts, including royal names, were generally well-known Canaanite or

Amorite patterns.[43] The article *h* which appears on the seals is used regularly also in the Tell Sīrān Inscription.

From Tell Sīrān comes additional evidence, masculine plurals in -*m* (versus Moabite), and the plurals *ywmt* and *šnt* with Phoenician and dialectal Hebrew, probably Israelite.

From Heshbon come a number of words with characteristic Canaanite phonemes: *ṣ'n* (*Aram. 'n'*) and *dš* (*Aram. dt'h*). Even more striking is the relative in *'š* elsewhere found only in Phoenician, but closely related to Northern Israelite *ša*-, Mishnaic *še*-, contrasting with Hebrew and Moabite *'aser* and older Canaanite *zū* (Ugaritic *dū*). The verb *ntn*, on the other hand, stands with Hebrew and Moabite (and presumably Proto-Semitic) against Phoenician and North Canaanite *ytn*. The survival of *'arḫu* "young cow" in Ammonite is remarkable, occurring elsewhere in Northwest Semitic, I believe, only in Ugaritic.

For all of its banal content, the Heshbon List proves an important addition to our knowledge of the Ammonite script and language.

## 2. *Heshbon Ostracon V* (Fig. 3 and Pl. I)

Ostracon V, Registry No. 1656, was found July 31, 1973, in Area B, Square 2, a context described by the excavator as Iron II/Persian. The right side of the sherd is missing certainly, and it may be that the inscription was incised (after firing) on an intact jar as a label of ownership.

The inscription can be reconstructed as follows:

*[ln]tn'l.*

An alternate reading, of course, would be *mtn'l. Ntn'l* is a popular biblical name, and *ntnyhw* appears both in the Bible and on

---

[43] To be sure, a number of names remain unexplained, including *dblbs* (*sic!*).

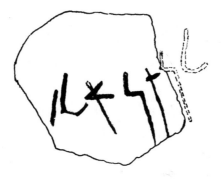

Fig. 3. A tracing of the Heshbon Ostracon V.

Hebrew seals. The Phoenician equivalent *ytn'l* is well known, as well as Phoenician *mtn'l, mtn'lm,* etc.

The letters of the graffito are skillfully made. They display the graceful, elongated forms of eighth-seventh century Ammonite. *Taw* is distinctive in that the cross-bar is tending to move to the right. A vertical stroke on the left of the name, evidently a word divider, suggests that a patronymic followed, now broken off. The graffito is probably to be assigned a seventh-century B.C. date.

### 3. *Heshbon Ostracon VI* (Pl. I)

Ostracon VI, Registry No. 1676, was found in Area C, Square 2. The archaeological context is predominantly Iron II/Persian with a few possible Iron I sherds present. The sherd preserves only a crude *'alep*.

### 4. *Heshbon Ostracon VII* (Pl. II)

Ostracon VII, Registry No. 1659, was found in Area B, Square 2, Locus 72, a context described as Iron II/Persian. While it shows unmistakable evidence of several lines of script, it is wholly illegible. It may be that at some future date new techniques will be developed to reveal script from faint traces, and this ostracon's secrets unlocked.

### 5. *Heshbon Ostracon VIII* (Pl. II)

Ostracon VIII, Registry No. 1658, was found in Area B, Square 2, in an Iron II/Persian context. Of the original script only traces remain, which are too indistinct to allow identifying any characters.

# A GREEK OSTRACON FROM HESHBON
## HESHBON OSTRACON IX

BASTIAAN VAN ELDEREN

Calvin Theological Seminary, Grand Rapids, Michigan

During the 1973 season at Heshbon an ostracon was found in Area B, Square 4, Locus 120W. The sherd has been identified as a Hellenistic body sherd by Dr. James Sauer, although the latest pottery found in the associated pottery pail was dated in the Early Roman period, with a mixture of Hellenistic and Iron Age body sherds. The registration number of the sherd is 1668, and its dimensions are 59 x 55 mm. (Pl. II).

There are traces of about 35 Greek letters on the sherd. However, only a few are in alignment, and there is no observable sequence of lines. Examination and experimentation have not produced any identifiable words or combinations. It would appear that this is possibly the product of someone's doodling or scribbling.

The following is a transcription of recognizable letters:

1       $a$   $\iota$       $o$

2         $\theta$ $\nu$ $\omega$ $\eta$

3            $\rho$   $\eta$   $\sigma$

4       $a$   $\overset{o}{\nu}$    $a\sigma$   $\gamma$   $o$   $\sigma$

5         $a\sigma$    $\kappa$   $\lambda$   $a$   $\rho$

*Along right side:*

6       $o$   $o$   $o$   $o$

7        $\rho$   $o$   $\sigma$

Palaeographically, some of the letter-forms on this ostracon can be paralleled in literary documents in the late Hellenistic period. The *alpha (ll. 1, 4), gamma (l. 4), ēta (ll. 2, 3), iota (l. 1), kappa (l. 5), rho (ll. 5, 7), sigma (ll. 4, 7), upsilon (l. 4), and ōmega (l. 2)* are the typical forms used in the second and first centuries B.C.[1] The dotted *thēta* in the ostracon *(l. 2)* is very common in third century documents.[2] However, some examples of the dotted *thēta* are found in the second and first centuries B.C.[3] Since the forms for the *alpha, sigma,* and *ōmega*[4] in the ostracon do not occur in the third century documents,[5] it appears that palaeographically the ostracon should be dated in the second or first centuries B.C. This would comport with the ceramic context of the ostracon cited above — late Hellenistic/early Roman.

[1] E. M. Thompson, *An Introduction to Greek and Latin Palaeography* (Oxford, 1912), pp. 144, 145.

[2] *Ibid.,* p. 144; C. H. Roberts, *Greek Literary Hands* (Oxford, 1956), no. 1 (4th cent.), no. 2a (1st half of 3d cent.); no. 3a (c. middle of 3d cent.); E. G. Turner, *Greek Manuscripts of the Ancient World* (Oxford, 1971), no. 51 (325-275 B.C.), no. 52 (early 3d cent.), no. 54 (middle 3d cent.).

[3] Thompson, *Introduction,* p. 145; Roberts, *Greek Literary Hands,* no. 6a (1st half of 2d cent. B.C.); Turner, *Greek Manuscripts,* no. 55 (middle of 1st cent. B.C.).

[4] Reading the second letter after the dotted *thēta* in line 2 on the ostracon as an *ōmega.*

[5] Cf. Roberts, *Greek Literary Hands,* numbers 1, 2a, 2b, 3a, 5a, 5b; Turner, *Greek Manuscripts,* numbers 40, 51, 52, 53, 54.

PLATE I

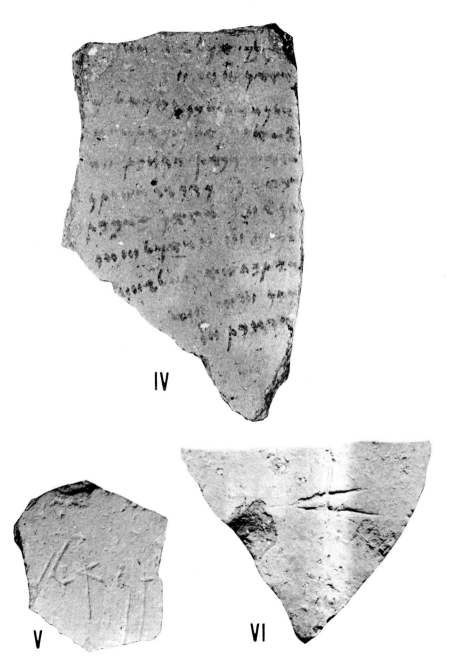

Ammonite Ostraca IV-VI from Heshbon (Actual size). Photos: Eugenia L. Nitowski.

PLATE II

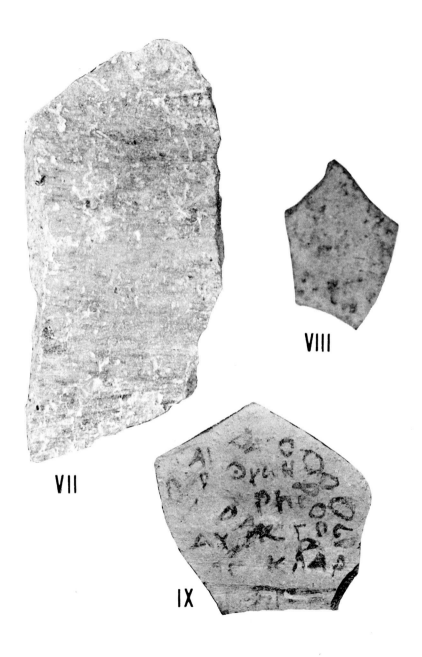

Ammonite Ostraca VII and VIII and Greek Ostracon IX from Heshbon
(Actual size). Photos: Eugenia L. Nitowski.